CIVIL WAR
BATON ROUGE,
PORT HUDSON
AND BAYOU SARA

D1526167

CIVIL WAR BATON ROUGE, PORT HUDSON AND BAYOU SARA

Capturing the Mississippi

DENNIS J. DUFRENE
SERIES EDITOR DOUG BOSTICK

Charleston   London

THE
History
PRESS

Published by The History Press
Charleston, SC 29403
www.historypress.net

Front cover: *The Battle of Baton Rouge, La. August 4th, 1862.* Published by Currier & Ives.

First published 2012

Manufactured in the United States

ISBN 978.1.60949.351.6

Library of Congress Cataloging-in-Publication Data
Dufrene, Dennis J.
Civil War Baton Rouge, Port Hudson and Bayou Sara : capturing the Mississippi / Dennis
J. Dufrene.
pages cm
Includes bibliographical references and index.
ISBN 978-1-60949-351-6
1. Louisiana--History--Civil War, 1861-1865--Campaigns. 2. Mississippi River Valley-
-History--Civil War, 1861-1865--Campaigns. 3. United States--History--Civil War,
1861-1865--Campaigns. 4. Baton Rouge (La.)--History--Siege, 1862. 5. Port Hudson (La.)-
-History--Siege, 1863. 6. Bayou Sara (La.)--History, Military--19th century. I. Title.
E474.1.D84 2012
973.7'3--dc23
2012001031

Dedicated to
Tweety & Myles
This book would not have been possible without their help and
understanding.

Contents

CONTENTS

Acknowledgements

I would like to thank the Louisiana State Historic Sites, in particular, Audubon State Historic Site and Port Hudson State Historic Site, for their time and effort. The staff at each site was a wealth of knowledge that was crucial to the completion of this book.

I would like to give a special thank-you to my family for their support and understanding. Without them, none of this would have been possible.

Introduction

The Civil War has been noted as the bloodiest war in American history, and rightfully so. Historians estimate that the War Between the States claimed the lives of more than 600,000 men, women and children. The Union and the Confederates faced each other more than ten thousand times over the course of four years. After each battle, skirmish and engagement, the surrounding landscape was scarred, never to be the same again. This scarring of the American landscape definitely holds true in the South, where most of the fighting took place.

Scores of books, articles and essays have been written to study and describe this nation-shaping event. Thousands of volumes lay on bookshelves that go into great detail on key battles such as the First Battle of Bull Run, Antietam, Shiloh and Gettysburg. There is not an author or historian alive who would disagree with the idea that if any of these key battles ended differently, the American Civil War could have had a vastly different outcome. Though these battles were important, the fate of the Civil War was not decided on these few battles alone.

The Civil War was made up of thousands of battles, though some were no larger than a skirmish. Each of these battles carried its own weight, contributing to the final outcome in its own way. Union and Confederate armies clashed all across the country, fighting in nooks and crannies sometimes not even big enough to warrant a name. This was definitely the case when the blue and gray went up against each other in Louisiana.

The two sides met on the field of battle throughout Louisiana at least twenty-three times over the four-year span of the war. Most of these battles or engagements were fought along the Mississippi River and the Red River. However, the Atchafalaya Basin and Bayou Lafourche had a considerable amount of action as well. Both the Confederacy and the Union realized that if either side controlled the waterways (and there were many), they could effectively control the state.

This was not to imply that Louisiana did not have any railroads. The state actually had twelve railroad companies that boasted several extensive lines and an array of smaller, rural ones. All in all, the companies had built nearly four hundred miles of track throughout the state. The most famous of the lines were the New Orleans, Jackson and Great Northern Railroad and the New Orleans, Opelousas and Great Western Railroad. Because of their strategic locations, the North and South were constantly vying for their control. These railroads were the pinnacle of transportation in their heyday. Besides the river, the railroad was the most efficient way to move men and supplies great distances, a fact that the rail men were proud to advertise. In 1861, a common advertisement for the New Orleans, Jackson and Great Northern Railroad read: "Two passenger trains leave the depot, at the corner of Callipe and Magnolia streets daily—the mail train at 7½ a.m. and the Express train at 7 p.m. Connections made with all the Northern and Eastern roads and tickets sold to all the principle cities, North East and West."

The ad also boasted that it was the quickest way to travel. Not only could you reach any major city in the country from the New Orleans, Jackson and Great Northern Railroad, but you could get there in record time. In 1861, it only took three days and sixteen hours to reach New York City.

Therefore, it is not any wonder that as the war loomed, the Confederacy began to utilize the rails extensively. And because of this extensive use, the railroad also became a target. The railroad was attacked many times. Colonel Clark Wright described one of these attacks in great detail: "I took out 1½ miles of wire, and burned it on top of three bridges I destroyed. I cut the road by tearing up the rails at three points. I burned out one culvert, and warped the rails materially at two points by building large fires on them. In the aggregate 1½ miles of road is destroyed and will require at least five or six days to repair it."

Another set of railroads, not as famous at the Great Northern or the Great Western, was the West Feliciana Railroad. The line was the first standard-gauge railroad built in the nation and spanned from Bayou Sara to Woodville, Mississippi. The railway was used primarily to transport cotton to and from the port in Bayou Sara to Woodville, which at the time was a major cotton hub in the South. The railroad's builder, Edward McGehee, said that traveling along Louisiana's dirt roads was "easy for a bird, practicable for a mule, but impossible for anything else." These railroads held a significant strategic value for transporting goods and troops, but they were only supplements to the vast network of waterways. This is especially true for the Mississippi River, which was the main thoroughfare into the nation's interior.

However, controlling the Mississippi River and the vast network of smaller waterways would be no easy task for either the Rebels or the Yankees. From the time it was a colony through the Civil War, Louisiana was known for its maze of rivers, lakes, bays and bayous. For decades, smugglers and pirates used the elusive waterways to traffic contraband and hide from authorities. Oftentimes, when Louisiana slaves would run away, they would hide in the dense wilderness, knowing that the swamps could easily conceal their presence. Unfortunately for these explorers, navigators, slaves and pirates, that wilderness was unforgiving. Many died along the rivers and bayous, especially when they were not prepared to deal with such a harsh environment.

Louisiana's rough terrain worked in favor of the Confederacy. As the Yankee troops worked their way up the river, many of the men were not prepared to travel through the dense swamps. Even when traveling up the Mississippi by boat, the hot, humid climate weighed heavy on the Northern troops. Even though the Rebels were often poorly supplied and poorly armed, at the very least, they were better acclimated to the harshness of the state's climate. Being unaccustomed to such heat, humidity and constant rainfall, many of the Union soldiers suffered a wide variety of ailments. It also seems that the Northerners never did get used to the extremes of Louisiana's climate. Even toward the end of the war in 1864, the men were still suffering. For example, when Nathanial Banks's men were occupying the town of Morganza, Louisiana, in 1864, much of his force was ill due to the climate. According to historian John Winters, "The heat and the excessive rainfall began to tell upon the troops…Epidemics of scurvy, chronic diarrhea, swamp fever [malaria], and smallpox began to take an appalling toll. Many times a day the death march sounded, and new victims were carried to their graves along the river bank."

Despite these adversities, the locals thrived in this climate. The meandering Mississippi River created some of the most fertile land in the country. North of Baton Rouge, Louisiana, cotton was king, and south of the city, sugar cane fields stretched for miles. These goods, among others, traveled up and down the river, creating bustling port cities in strategic locations on the riverbanks. Places such as Bayou Sara and Port Hudson were hot spots for trade prior to the Civil War. However, the war nearly wiped these towns off the map. The most famous port city in Louisiana, New Orleans, survived the war, but it took a toll on its trade and commerce. As for the state's capital, Baton Rouge, it did not so much survive but rather endured. It, too, was nearly wiped off the map. It is certain that when the state's officials decided to secede from the Union, they did not expect the Union's attempt to capture the Mississippi River to take such a toll on their prominent cities along its banks.

Chapter 1

Louisiana Secedes

Over the course of 1860, Louisiana faced the same political instability that was running rampant through much of the nation. The state was at a political crossroads. Most Louisianans were content with their position in the Union. Many of the state's residents hoped that Louisiana could remain neutral if war did break out. This was largely due to the fact that even though large plantations did thrive throughout the state, Louisiana also relied heavily on trade and commerce as a source of income. New Orleans was the largest city in the South, and it was also an international center of commerce, distributing goods up the Mississippi River, as well as out to the Gulf of Mexico. Farther north on the Mississippi River, the town of Bayou Sara was quickly becoming an important hub for commerce as well. It was one of the larger port cities between New Orleans and Vicksburg, Mississippi.

However, the idea of neutrality quickly changed during two key elections. One of these was when Thomas Overton Moore was elected as Louisiana's governor. The planters held a considerable amount of power in Louisiana, and they were concerned with the political changes that were taking place across the country. They set out to elect a governor who would reflect their interests, and Moore was anything but shy about his position on states' rights and a liberal federal government. Therefore, the second key election was when Abraham Lincoln, who was labeled as a liberal presidential candidate, was elected president of the United States in the 1860 election. Lincoln attempted to reassure southerners that their rights would be maintained by stating in his inaugural address, "Apprehension seems to exist among the people of the Southern States that by the accession of a Republican

Abraham Lincoln. *Courtesy of Library of Congress, Prints and Photographs Division.*

Administration, their property, and their peace, and personal security, are to be endangered. There has never been any reasonable cause for such apprehension." Nevertheless, it appeared that Louisiana was destined to secede from the Union.

In December 1860, South Carolina was the first state to secede from the Union and claim its independence. Many within the state of Louisiana felt that their state should do the same. There was no other Louisiana citizen who shared this sentiment more than Governor Thomas Moore. Moore was the son of a Carolina planter family. As an adult, he managed his uncle's plantation and went on to own his own cotton plantation in Rapides Parish. Being successful in agriculture, Moore had the funds to try his hand at politics. It seems that Moore had a knack for politics and quickly rose to power in Louisiana. He was elected to the House of Representatives in 1848 and then to the Senate in 1856. Three years later, he was able to defeat Thomas Jefferson Wells and become governor of Louisiana in 1859.

Moore never hid his belief that Louisiana, along with the rest of the South, would be better off if it broke away from the Union. When he was sworn in, he made his opinion very clear when he stated that owning slaves was a "social and political blessing." Furthermore, the governor felt that federal government was working to revoke the rights of southern slaveholders, and many plantation owners agreed with him. This feeling toward the federal government is somewhat ironic. Three years prior to Moore's inauguration, Republican abolitionists were making claims that southern planters had infiltrated the Supreme Court. These claims were mainly due to their 7–2 decision in favor of slavery in the Dred Scott case. Nevertheless, Moore made his intentions clear during his inauguration speech when he stated, "At the North, a wide spread sympathy with felons

Governor Thomas Moore. *Courtesy of Duke University Digital Collections.*

has deepened the distrust in the permanent Government, and awakened sentiments favorable to a separation of the states."

However, not everyone was for secession. Many southerners felt that something must be done but secession was too drastic of a move. A young Sarah Morgan conveys those feelings in her diary when she writes:

> *I was never a Secessionist, for I quietly adopted father's views on political subjects without meddling with them. But even father went over with his State, and when so many outrages were committed by the fanatical leaders of the North, though he regretted the Union, said, "Fight to the death for our liberty." I say so, too. I want to fight until we win the cause so many have died for. I don't believe in Secession, but I do in Liberty. I want the South to conquer, dictate its own terms, and go back to the Union, for I believe that, apart, inevitable ruin awaits both. It is a rope of sand, this Confederacy, founded on the doctrine of Secession, and will not last many years—not five. The North cannot subdue us. We are too determined to*

be free. They have no right to confiscate our property to pay debts they themselves have incurred. Death as a nation, rather than Union on such terms. We will have our rights secured on so firm a basis that it can never be shaken. If by power of overwhelming numbers they conquer us, it will be a barren victory over a desolate land.

Those feelings aside, it was no surprise that barely even two months after Lincoln's election, Louisiana chose to secede from the Union. Moore's goal was to secede from the Union before Lincoln took office in March 1861. In preparation for this secession, Moore ordered all U.S. military posts to be seized by the state militia on January 10, 1861. While the posts were being seized, Moore held a state convention to determine if Louisiana would leave the Union. The vote was necessary because not everyone in Louisiana was keen on leaving the Union. Those numbers were small. It is estimated that pro-secession delegates outnumbered Unionist delegates at least two to one; however, it is still unclear if that was by design on the part of Governor Moore. When the vote was cast, the outcome was clear. It was a landslide: 113 in favor of seceding and 17 against.

The legislature made its decision official on January 26, 1861, though it is believed that the decision was made long before the votes were cast. A portion of the ordinance of secession reads as follows:

We, the people of the State of Louisiana, in convention assembled, do declare and ordain, and it is hereby declared and ordained, That the ordinance passed by us in convention on the 22d day of November, in the year eighteen hundred and eleven, whereby the Constitution of the United States of America and the amendments of the said Constitution were adopted, and all laws and ordinances by which the State of Louisiana became a member of the Federal Union, be, and the same are hereby, repealed and abrogated; and that the Union now subsisting between Louisiana and other States under the name of "The United States of America" is hereby dissolved.

Newspapers chronicled the day as one of celebration. The *Baton Rouge Gazette* described the scene with great fanfare, with legislators and local citizens parading their new flag, the Pelican Flag, along with firing rockets and guns in celebration of their new independence. This celebration would prove to be premature when Union troops come knocking at Baton Rouge's door.

Chapter 2

The Union Plan for the Mississippi River

As soon as Lincoln and his advisors received word that Louisiana had seceded from the Union, they knew what must be done: the Union had to capture the Mississippi River. Being the main thoroughfare into the interior of America, the Mississippi River was considered to be one of the most critical theaters of the Civil War. This idea was not lost on the Confederates, either. The newly elected president of the Confederacy, Jefferson Davis, described Vicksburg as a "vital point" in the lower Mississippi Valley.

The Union plan, proposed by General in Chief Winfield Scott, was deceptively simple: create a blockade in the Gulf of Mexico to block the flow of resources to and from the South. Once the blockade was in place, the Union would then travel north up the Mississippi while also traveling south down the Mississippi. This maneuver would not only divide the South but also effectively strangle the region by restricting the movement of men, weapons and supplies. This plan was adopted in 1862 and became known as the Anaconda Plan in newspapers across the country.

The plan was a tremendous success, and its implementation was a critical factor in the outcomes of the Western Campaign. By April 24, 1862, Federal captain (later admiral) David Glasgow Farragut, coming from the south, forced the city of New Orleans to surrender. With the Crescent City under Federal control, the Union could move freely down the Mississippi River from New Orleans into the Gulf of Mexico. The Union also maintained control over the river north to right above Vicksburg. Along with Vicksburg, there was only about forty miles of river left for the Union to capture. The Confederates controlled the river from Louisiana's capital city of Baton

Left: Winfield Scott. *Courtesy of the U.S. Post Office.*

Below: Anaconda Plan. *Courtesy of Library of Congress, Prints and Photographs Division.*

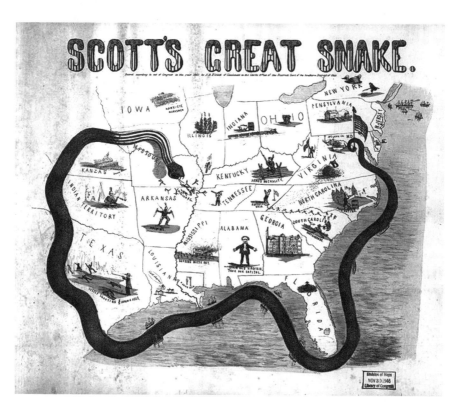

Rouge stretching north to the little river town of Bayou Sara, which is now part of modern-day St. Francisville.

Though the area is commonly overshadowed by the Vicksburg Campaign, the forty miles that lie between Baton Rouge and Bayou Sara were a hotbed of battles, skirmishes, engagements and affairs. From the summer of 1862 through the summer of 1863, the region was scarred by musket balls and cannon fire, all in an attempt to capture the Mississippi River between Baton Rouge and Bayou Sara.

Today, this area is composed of three parishes: East Baton Rouge, East Feliciana and West Feliciana. Several skirmishes were fought in outlying areas that were located in Assumption, Ascension, Pointe Coupee and West Baton Rouge Parishes. The Confederates fought hard to keep the river out of Union hands; however, they were only delaying the inevitable. Just as New Orleans, the largest city in the South during the Civil War, was crucial to control the river from the Crescent City to the Gulf of Mexico, the small river community of Port Hudson, along with Baton Rouge, was key in securing the river from New Orleans north up to Vicksburg. The difference between New Orleans and Port Hudson is that New Orleans fell to Union troops after only six days, whereas it took the Union forty-eight days to take Port Hudson.

Baton Rouge is located on the east side of the Mississippi River and nestled on the first series of bluffs. These bluffs mark where the state's highlands end and the flat delta plain begins. The city is roughly sixty miles inland from the Gulf of Mexico, and its subtropical climate, which is usually free of various temperature extremes, makes the area ideal for growing sugar cane. The city of Baton Rouge was very unique when compared to other southern cities of the time. Mark Twain wrote:

> Baton Rouge was clothed in flowers, like a bride—no, much more so; like a greenhouse. For we were in the absolute South now—no modifications, no compromises, no half-way measures. The magnolia trees in the Capitol grounds were lovely and fragrant, with their dense rich foliage and huge snowball blossoms...We were certainly in the South at last; for here the sugar region begins, and the plantations—vast green levels, with sugar-mill and negro quarters clustered together in the middle distance—were in view.

Sugar cane and cotton were the lifeblood of the region and shaped Baton Rouge over time. By 1846, the Louisiana state legislature was dominated in number by rural planters. These planters were able to move the seat of

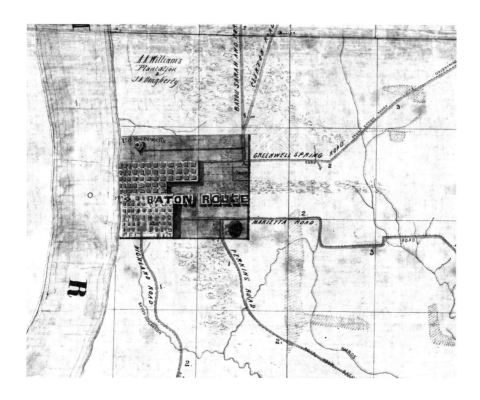

Above: An 1863 map of Baton Rouge. *Courtesy of Library of Congress, Geography and Map Division.*

Below: Baton Rouge Pentagon Barracks. *Courtesy of Library of Congress, Prints and Photographs Division.*

the government from New Orleans to Baton Rouge. These crops gave the planters a considerable amount of power not only in the South but across the globe. Tons of cotton passed through the port of New Orleans and on to Europe, which had become dependent on this crop—so much so that when the Southern states seceded from the Union, they withheld much of this crop in order to force Europe to recognize the Confederacy as independent.

Because of its high demand, cotton could easily be converted into gold, not only for the Confederates but for the Federals as well. There were several battles throughout the region that started because the Union was trying to confiscate more of the crop. This became such an issue that the Confederacy had a long-standing policy throughout the war: whatever cotton that could not be transported would be burned to keep it out of the hands of the Union. It was not uncommon to see ten to twenty thousand bales of cotton lit on fire as Confederate troops retreated from an engagement.

Burning was not the only way the Confederates attempted to keep cotton away from the Union. Early on, at the start of the war, the Confederacy created a policy that outlawed the exportation of cotton to the Union. The idea behind this policy was to starve out the Yankee textile factories so those goods could not be traded with Europe. The concern was that any funds acquired through European trade would certainly be used in the war effort. The Confederacy did try to monopolize the cotton trade but could not keep the crop completely out of the hands of its opponents. By raiding port cities and seizing crops from abandoned or even occupied plantations, the Union was able to acquire tons of cotton. This cotton was commonly sold at auction, and the funds were, of course, used to further the war effort.

Baton Rouge, Louisiana: The Old State Capital Castle. *Early twentieth-century postcard.*

The Union acquisition of cotton was not the only problem the Confederacy had to deal with in terms of trade. Since the Confederacy outlawed the selling of cotton to the Union, it was solely reliant on Europe to buy the crop. However, the Union made it more difficult for the Confederacy to trade with Europe because of the Union blockade of 1861. This restricted movement of cotton, either into the Union or Europe, created a cash flow problem for the Confederacy.

The other cash crop in Louisiana was sugar cane. Grown predominantly in south Louisiana, the crop was often described as "a prize more precious than rubies." Cane country stretched from the Red River to the Gulf of Mexico and encompassed areas of the Atchafalaya, Bayou Lafourche and of course the Mississippi River. All in all, sugar cane was grown in twenty-four parishes prior to the Civil War. The crop was so extensively grown that it was not unheard of to have entire military companies made up solely of sugar planters. This was definitely true for the artillery regiment known as the St. Mary Cannoneers. Today, only about 60 sugarhouses remain out of the 1,291 in production on the eve of the Civil War.

The topography of the region has changed immensely since it saw the bloodshed of the Civil War more than 150 years ago. Where woodlands and plantations once stood now stand industrial facilities and interstate highways. Little remains of the terrain's former self, which has been altered in the name of progress. Presently, a few historic buildings and structures have been restored or maintained that can give one a glimpse into the area's tumultuous past.

Such structures are the Old State Capitol, Pentagon Barracks and Magnolia Cemetery. Magnolia Cemetery was the site of the Battle of Baton Rouge, after which many soldiers were simply buried where they died. Nevertheless, sites such as these are only tiny windows into the past. Even the mighty Mississippi River does not look as it did during the Civil War. Over time, the muddy waters that were sometimes referred to as "inland seas" have been channeled and engineered in an attempt to tame the floodwaters that were responsible for making the area so fertile. Once the river was tamed, it allowed the banks of the river to be inundated with urban sprawl and commercial construction.

Going backward in time, we can only imagine how Mark Twain felt when he said, "It is not a commonplace river, but on the contrary is in all ways remarkable."

Chapter 3

The Union Blockade

In an effort to execute the Anaconda Plan, the Union had to travel north up the Mississippi River in order to bisect the Confederacy. This bisection of the South would rely heavily on the success of the Union navy, which in Louisiana was commanded by Admirals David G. Farragut and David D. Porter. Before making their way to Baton Rouge from the south and then on to Bayou Sara, the admirals had to start their campaign at the mouth of the Mississippi. The first step in their campaign was to stifle trade and commerce through the use of a naval blockade.

Abraham Lincoln played an important role in the overall success of the navy when he ordered the Union blockade in 1861. The blockade stretched to include nearly 3,500 miles of Confederate coastline, shutting down twelve major ports, one of which was New Orleans. This blockade was one of the first Union naval activities that Louisiana had to deal with, but it definitely was not the last. The blockade was maintained throughout the war and was not lifted until 1865. This blockade, just as most of the other naval operations conducted in Louisiana, is thought of as one of the most important naval activities executed by the Union during the war.

The Crescent City was one of the largest cotton exporters in the South and a major center of commerce for the Confederacy. This blockade considerably hampered trade in New Orleans and across the South. Lincoln issued a proclamation of blockade on April 19, 1861. The president cited the fact that the Confederacy was taking on volunteer vessels to act as privateers and attack Union ships. These Confederate attacks were usually on trade vessels and not naval ships. Therefore, Lincoln ordered the blockade to stretch from South Carolina to Texas. Then, just over a week later, Lincoln extended the proclamation to cover Virginia and North Carolina. With the blockade in effect, New Orleans struggled to export or import goods. Many of the privateers who signed on to harass Union shipping found a new niche: breaking through the blockade in order to ship goods.

Though hampered, trade continued. The Confederacy employed small, fast-sailing ships, known as blockade runners, to smuggle goods past the Union and out to neutral ports in the Caribbean. Even though the Union deployed five hundred ships to patrol the coastal waters, the area was too vast for them to stamp out Confederate trade completely. It has been estimated that the blockade runners were successful more than 80 percent of the time. However, the lighter ships could only carry small loads of cargo at a time. Therefore, even with their high success rate, the blockade runners could only move a small fraction of goods.

Aside from slowing trade and stamping out Southern privateers, the blockade played another important role. Though frustrated by the proclamation, many Confederate leaders saw it as a formal recognition of their independence and an act of war toward their fledging nation. When Brigadier General Braxton Bragg, in Pensacola, received official word of the blockade, he called it "a virtual acknowledgement of our national existence and independence." This is due to the fact that in the past, nations did not blockade their own ports. They simply would just close them off. Nevertheless, Lincoln never officially recognized existence of any such independence in his efforts to keep the Union whole.

The blockade also forced several other countries to force their hands and make a move that would provide the Union with some idea on where these nations stood when it came to any sort of alliance. Lincoln received his answers within the next two months. Both Great Britain and France declared their neutrality in May and June, respectively. Many within the Union believed that this European neutrality was the countries' subtle yet unofficial way of recognizing the Confederacy as an independent nation. However, it is more likely that Great Britain and France wanted to remain neutral for the same reasons that many Louisianans wanted to prior to the outbreak of the war.

By maintaining their neutrality, Great Britain and France were both able to trade with the North and the South. The countries did this by setting up and maintaining neutral ports in the Caribbean. Most of the trade was conducted on the islands of Bermuda, the Bahamas, Havana or Cuba. As long as the blockade runners did not get caught, Great Britain and France would still receive their steady flow of cotton, turpentine or tobacco. In return, the Confederacy would receive a wide variety of manufactured and luxury goods, such as rifles, medicine, brandy, lingerie and even coffee. The wealthy located in these blockaded areas would pay a hefty price for these luxuries. The blockade runners could charge anywhere from $300 to upward of $1,000 per ton of cargo that made it to the docks. A blockade runner only making two round trips per month could easily bring in over $170,000 per month after expenses and wages were paid. To put that number in perspective, that is the equivalent of more than $400,000 per month today.

An example of a typical load for a blockade runner was the cargo of the *William G. Hewes*. The *Hewes* was a 747-ton iron side-wheel steamship built in Wilmington, Delaware, for commercial service in 1860. However, it was seized by the State of Louisiana in April 1861 and used as a blockade runner. The ship's name was changed in 1863, and shortly thereafter, it was seized by the Federal navy. It was discovered that the ship was carrying Austrian rifles, salt, beef, paper, saltpeter and a number of Confederate dispatches.

With trade reduced significantly and privateering kept to a minimum, the Union navy was able to set its sights on New Orleans. However, the Union navy had to sail up the river for nearly one hundred miles before reaching the Crescent City. Along the way, the Federals fought their way past several forts. Unfortunately for the Rebels, this would prove to be an easy task for the formidable Union navy. Yet before the Yankees could make it up the river, the Confederates executed a raid in the mouth of the Mississippi near an area called Head of Passes. Though the Union was confident, this defensive effort made by the Rebels proved that capturing the Mississippi River would be no easy task.

Chapter 4
The Battle of Head of Passes

The Confederates did not take the Union blockade lightly. Not only did the Rebels use blockade runners, but they also executed a naval raid on a blockade squadron anchored near Head of Passes at the mouth of the Mississippi River. The raiders consisted of six gunboats and an ironclad. The Confederates also had three fire rafts at their disposal. These rafts were towed behind the ironclad the CSS *Manassas*. Commodore George N. Hollins commanded this small fleet, which was known as the Mosquito Fleet.

Hollins was an experienced sailor and had participated in his fair share of blockade running. When he was only fifteen years old, the young Hollins served on the *Erie* as a midshipman when it was making its attempt to break the British blockade of Chesapeake Bay in 1814. Throughout most of his adult life, Hollins moved up the ranks in the United States Navy. By 1861, he had achieved the rank of captain. In March of that year, he attempted to resign his commission, but his superiors refused the resignation and ordered Captain Hollins's arrest. He was able to avoid capture and found himself in the South. The former captain was asked to consult with the Confederate leaders on the creation of a navy for the Confederacy. As the leaders were impressed with his record, Hollins was made a commander in the Confederate navy. The commander continued to impress his superiors. By July 1861, he was in charge of a naval station near New Orleans.

The Mosquito Fleet was composed of three ships: USS *Vincennes*, USS *Preble* and USS *Richmond*. The *Vincennes* was a 703-ton Boston-class sloop of war. Not only did the ship boast eighteen guns, but it was the first U.S. warship to circumnavigate the world. The USS *Preble* was a sloop of war with sixteen guns at its disposal. However, it was the USS *Richmond* that proved to be the Mosquito Fleet's biggest challenge. The flagship was a 225-foot behemoth that displaced over 2,600 tons.

The *Richmond*'s armament consisted of one eighty-pound Dahlgren smoothbore, one twenty-pound Dahlgren smoothbore and one thirty-pound Parrott rifle. The small squadron was a formidable armada by itself. Though the flagship was an intimidating sight, its commander was a little less intimidating. The *Richmond* was captained by John Pope. He was a capable leader for the most part, but he had just finished going up against the CSS *Ivy* three days prior. Also, after the Battle at Head of Passes, he was relieved of duty at his own request due to health issues. Whether these health issues played a major role in Pope's ineptness will never be known. Unfortunately for the Federals, no matter what was the cause, this ineptness would come back to haunt the Union.

Captain Pope was not the only problem the Union squadron had to deal with. There were several drawbacks to the other ships. For example, the drawback of the *Vincennes* and the *Preble* is that they were only powered with sails. Therefore, they often required the towing assistance of the *Water Witch*, a side-wheel steamer. Even though the *Water Witch* was mainly used for its towing capabilities, it boasted an impressive array of guns as well. The *Water Witch* carried four thirty-two-pounders, one twelve-pound smoothbore and one twenty-pound Parrott rifle.

When the Mosquito squadron caught the Federals anchored off Head of Passes, the Confederate commander had a plan. Hollins's plan was to use the ironclad *Manassas* to destroy the USS *Richmond*. Then, once the *Richmond* was out of the way, a signal would be given and three of the gunboats would ignite and push the fire rafts into the remaining ships of the Union fleet. He would execute his plan on October 12, 1861.

On the morning of October 12, the *Preble* caught sight of the *Manassas* during its initial approach and immediately fired on the Confederate ironclad. Commander Henry French of the *Preble* described this sighting in his official report:

> *The moon had set, or was obscured by clouds, and the night somewhat dark, with the wind from the northward. As I passed out of my cabin on my way to the deck I saw through the port an indescribable object not 20 yards distant from our quarter, moving with great velocity toward the bow of the* Richmond. *My orders from the senior officer were in the event of discovering any danger at night to hoist a red light at the gaff. This had*

been done by the officer of the deck, instantly, on the discovery of the object, which was first seen about 15 or 20 feet directly ahead of this ship, and drifting with the current directly towards us; not a speck of light, smoke, or any moving thing could be seen on or in it, and it looked somewhat like a huge whale in the water. The instant the persons on board of it discovered our movements it seemed to change its direction to avoid us and make directly for the Richmond.

The Federal gunship overshot its fast-moving target, and the *Manassas* was able to sail past the *Preble*. With a clear shot heading toward the *Richmond*, the *Manassas* sailed ahead. The *Richmond* was taking on coal and was lashed to the coal schooner *Joseph H. Toone*. Because of its quick maneuvering and the *Richmond*'s vulnerable position, the *Manassas* was able to inflict a glancing blow to the Federal sloop of war. The blow not only damaged the *Richmond* but the engines of the *Manassas* as well.

As the Confederate ironclad limped away, the crew signaled for the release of the fire rafts. The flaming rafts sent meandering down the river threw the Union crewmen into a panic. Even though chaos ran free on board the Union ships, they were still able to fire upon the *Manassas* and even scored a hit. The hit struck the stacks of the ironclad, knocking one of them down. The Rebel gunships made good use of the chaos and fired on the Union fleet. A chase ensued that ended with the entire Union fleet, with the exception of the *Preble*, grounded. With the powerful *Richmond* grounded, the Mosquito Fleet fired, making sure to keep slightly out of range of the ship's smoothbores.

The two fleets blasted away at each other for hours; however, neither side sustained any considerable damage. The Confederate fleet was able to sail away unscathed, while the *Richmond* took on two hits, neither of them causing any real damage to the floating behemoth. Running low on coal and ammunition, the Mosquito Fleet ended the attack and sailed back upriver to Fort Jackson.

This raid did not stop the Federal advance up the Mississippi River, but it was able to slow it down. That in itself was a small victory for the Confederates and was able to buy New Orleans just a little more time. More importantly for the Confederacy, it was the first of many naval battles that the Confederates had to face in Louisiana, and they were off to a promising start. After his victory at Head of Passes, Hollins was appointed flag officer and sent to Columbus, Kentucky, only to be called back to New Orleans six months later.

Chapter 5

Forts Jackson and St. Philip

A s it traveled up the Mississippi River, the Union navy found little resistance until it reached Forts Jackson and St. Philip. It had long been believed by the Union that the two forts were invulnerable to its naval guns. However, Commander David Dixon Porter had a plan. Using branches and brush collected from the riverbank, Porter ordered his men to camouflage the twenty mortar schooners. The disguised flotilla was anchored near the river's banks during the early morning hours of April 18.

The use of the camouflage was short-lived because Porter ordered the bombardment of the forts on the same day. The commander's goal was to reduce the two forts to rubble. It has been estimated that the flotilla fired nearly three thousand shells on that day. According to the *Official Records of the Union and Confederate Navies in the War of the Rebellion*, Brigadier General Duncan, Confederate commander in charge of the two forts, described the damage to Fort Jackson:

> *The quarters in the bastions were fired and burned down early in the day, as well as the quarters immediately without the fort. The citadel was set on fire and extinguished several times during the first part of the day, but later it became impossible to put out the flames, so that when the enemy ceased firing it was one burning mass, greatly endangering the magazines, which at one time were reported to be on fire. Many of the men and most of the officers lost their bedding and clothing by these fires, which greatly added to the discomforts of the overflow. The mortar fire was accurate and terrible, many of the shells falling everywhere within the fort and disabling some of our best guns.*

Porter would later write about the bombardment in a letter to a friend:

> *The results of our mortar practice here have exceeded anything I ever dreamed of; and for my success I am mainly indebted to the accuracy of positions marked down, under Mr. Gerdes' direction, by Mr. Harris and Mr. Oltmanns. They made a minute and complete survey from the "jump" to the forts, most of the time exposed to fire from shot and shell, and from sharpshooters from the bushes…The position that every vessel was to occupy was marked by a white flag, and we knew to a yard the exact distance of the hole in the mortar from the forts…Mr. Oltmanns and Mr. Harris remained constantly on board to put the vessels in position again when they had to haul off for repairs, or on account of the severity of the enemy's fire…I assure you that I shall never undertake a bombardment unless I have them at my side.*

Aside from the damage the mortars inflicted on the first day, the two forts still stood. Though the rate of fire was reduced, the bombardment continued for the next five days. The constant bombardment was depleting the ammunition stores at a tremendous rate. It also appeared that the Confederates showed no sign of surrender. Though the Federal barrage made it difficult for the Rebels to return fire, they did so as often as they could. The steadfastness of the Confederates forced Admiral Farragut to make a decision. Feeling as though he could no longer wait on Porter's flotilla to subdue the two forts, Farragut decided to make a run past the forts.

Farragut rearranged his fleet into three sections and attempted his run in the early morning hours of April 24. The goal was to use the darkness and smoke to obscure the aim of the Confederate guns. Also, Farragut ordered his men not to stop to return any fire. He ordered his ships to

Admiral David G. Farragut. *Courtesy of Library of Congress.*

33

maintain the course and return fire but pass those forts as quickly as possible. The admiral ordered his ships to sail upriver in two columns: the starboard column fired on Fort St. Philip, while the port column fired on Fort Jackson.

Just as Farragut had hoped, the Confederate guns could not hit their mark. However, neither could his men. The darkness, along with the smoke and the speed that his ships were moving, made it very difficult for the Union navy to cause any significant damage to the forts. Also, the chaos made it difficult for the men inside the forts to determine the difference between Union navy and Confederate navy. This rendered the Confederate navy useless. The Confederates were forced to protect themselves not only from Union fire but also from the fire of Fort Jackson and Fort St. Philip. This forced the Confederate navy to pull back and remain out of range of the forts' guns.

Farragut's fleet made it past the two forts and sustained little damage; however, it still had to battle the Confederates who lay in wait for them just above the forts. The Confederates believed that the CSS *Louisiana* would be able to defend the river from any Union attack. Unfortunately for the Rebels, the *Louisiana* was not ready for battle. Its crew was not well trained, and the ironclad had issues with its engines and guns. With no plan and lack of communication, the Confederate defense of the river turned into a series of ship-to-ship battles. The Union was able to either outfight or outrun most of the Confederate ships. The only Union ship lost was the USS *Varuna*. The *Varuna* was chased down by the CSS *Governor Moore* and eventually rammed by it. The *Varuna* was able to reach the shallows but still partially sank. Overall, the Confederates lost twelve ships, including the celebrated *Louisiana*. However, the *Louisiana* was not lost due to the battle. During the surrender of the fleet and forts, its captain, Alexander F. Warley, felt that the terms of surrender did not apply to him and his crew. Therefore, rather than losing the ship, Warley sailed the ship upriver and ordered it to be scuttled. The crew did as ordered and set fire to the *Louisiana*. The flaming ship floated downriver and, either by design or coincidence, exploded as it neared Fort St. Philip. The ship still carried enough in its magazine to cause the blast to kill one of the soldiers at the fort.

Farragut's fleet successfully made it past Forts Jackson and St. Philip. With the surrender of the forts negotiated by Nathaniel Banks, the Union had successfully seized control of the Mississippi River south of New Orleans. The admiral was only seventy-five miles away from New Orleans.

Alexander F. Warley believed that the terms of the surrender did not apply to his ship because he believed the surrender of Fort Jackson was a result of mutiny and betrayal. The night before the surrender of the fort, the garrison inside began to fear the worst. The *Louisiana* was not the savior of New Orleans. Then the rhetoric became even worse as rumors and stories began to spread of the fall of New Orleans. The city was already being evacuated by the railway, and the men feared that they would be sacrificed so that the town would have time to evacuate as many as possible.

By midnight, the fear and rumors became too much. Most of the garrison broke out into a full-scale revolt. The men ransacked the fort, spiking the guns as they came across them. Many of the men did not even bother spiking the guns. They simply deserted the fort. Many of the deserters had wives and family members living at Quarantine Station. Long before the bombardment, Duncan had ordered the men to stay in the fort and ordered that the wives and families of the men were not allowed inside. Therefore, the families lived in the closest possible location to the fort, Quarantine Station.

When officers attempted to stop the troops in revolt, the ranks fired at them, forcing them to pull back. It seemed as though the entire fort was plunged into madness, except for the St. Mary Cannoneers. The Cannoneers, officially known as 1st Battery Volunteer Artillery, were mustered into Confederate service at Franklin, Louisiana, on October 7, 1861. The heavy artillerists were the only unit that did not mutiny on that night. The officers and enlisted men became prisoners of war when the forts surrendered the following morning. They remained prisoners of war until mid-1862. After receiving their release, the men gathered at Camp Hunter to be outfitted again as a field battery.

It has been estimated that there were somewhere between 250 to 300 mutineers who ran amuck in Fort Jackson that night. Many of those men forced their way out of the fort, ran straight into General Butler's pickets and immediately surrendered themselves to the Federals. Many of the men were paroled, believe it or not, against their will. Their concern was that they would simply be drafted back into the Confederate army and forced to fight or, worse, punished for the crime of mutiny. Instead, many of these men swore allegiance to the Union, according to a report from the *New York Evening Post*. The reporter writes, "To-day we administered the oath of allegiance to our prisoners, and let them go. They all took it willingly and apparently gladly. What do you think of two squads of them, about seventy-five men each, volunteering three cheers for the Union and giving them with a will?"

There were several other news stories touting the same types of accounts. However, many Confederate leaders challenged these accounts, claiming that these stories of Confederate men changing sides and swearing allegiance to the Union was nothing more than propaganda being used to break the Rebels' morale. Whether these were true or not was irrelevant. Fort Jackson had fallen.

Chapter 6

The Fall of New Orleans and the Scuttling of the USS *Barataria*

Once the Union made it past Forts Jackson and St. Philip, there was nothing to stop it from taking New Orleans. The Union troops simply marched off their boats and into the Crescent City. Not a single gunshot was fired. This was by no means due to any cowardice on behalf of the Rebels. On the contrary, the act of surrendering actually saved the city.

New Orleans's position on the river, along with its bowl-like terrain, made it a nightmare to defend. This allowed the Union navy to keep the "high ground" while never leaving the river. They simply aimed their guns down into the bowl. Furthermore, if any section of the levee was to be destroyed, the river would just flow down into the bowl and flood the city. Destroying New Orleans would have taken very little effort by the Union. However, the city remained intact. Intact or not, many Louisiana citizens openly criticized the Confederacy for losing the Crescent City so easily. An example of such a criticism by Ed G. Randolph states:

> *You will know that I am not disposed to rashly criticize or censure the acts of our leaders—because we cannot always know or be informed of the facts or true situation but it does seem to me that there was a screw loose somewhere. We should have had one of our very best soldiers commanding at a port of so much importance as that of New Orleans and vicinity. New Orleans was of first importance and ought to have been held at all hazards it would have been better far better to have given up Charleston, Savanah and also Mobile. Concentrating the forces and the munitions for the safety of New Orleans. But Alas why talk of it now. Surely there must have been treachery somewhere.*

The fact that New Orleans remained intact is a surprising detail in the Union mission to control the river because when the Yankees occupied the Crescent City, they were not welcomed with open arms. When Captain Bailey, of the USS *Cayuga*, was sent to New Orleans to accept the surrender, he was met with an angry and increasingly violent mob. His men were not even allowed to raise the Union flag over the city. When the Union flag was finally raised over the New Orleans Mint, angry citizens tore down the flag from the pole and ripped it to shreds. Normally, Admiral Farragut would have leveled any who defied him in such a way. Yet, luckily for the Crescent City, Farragut had his sights set on the rest of the Mississippi.

Though the city itself was spared, the citizens of New Orleans were forced to endure the rule of Major General Benjamin Butler. Butler quickly gained the nickname "Beast" by the residents of New Orleans, largely due to decisions he made. One of those decisions was the highly controversial Women's Order. Upon the arrival of the Union men, the women of New Orleans were less than hospitable to the Yankee occupiers. They would not only curse the soldiers, but they would go as far as to taunt and spit on the men. One woman emptied her chamber pot on the head of Admiral Farragut.

General Benjamin Butler. *Courtesy of Library of Congress, Prints and Photographs Division.*

The women hoped that their retaliation would spark the men to revolt. However, it only sparked Butler to issue General Order No. 28. The order stated:

> As the officers and soldiers of the United States have been subjected to repeated insults from the women (calling themselves ladies) of New Orleans, in return for the most scrupulous noninterference and courtesy on our part, it is ordered that hereafter when any female shall, by word, gesture, or movement, insult or show contempt for any officer or soldier of the United States, she shall be regarded and held liable to be treated as a woman of the town plying her avocation.

Though the order had its intended effect and the insults from the women of New Orleans stopped, it created a backlash of opposition not only across the South but across Europe as well. In response to this order, Governor Moore wrote:

> The annals of warfare between civilized nations afford no similar instance of infamy to this order. It is thus proclaimed to the world that the exhibition of any disgust or repulsiveness by the women of New Orleans to the hated invaders of their home and the slayers of their fathers, brothers, and husbands shall constitute a justification to a brutal soldiery for the indulgence of their lust.

Moore's letter goes on to urge the men of New Orleans to revolt. Jefferson Davis, the president of the Confederate States, wrote a proclamation of his own, calling for the execution of Butler. In his proclamation, Davis states:

> I…declare the said Benjamin F. Butler to be a felon, deserving of capital punishment. I do order that he be no longer considered or treated simply as a public enemy of the Confederate States of America, but as an outlaw and common enemy of mankind, and that in the event of his capture the officer in command of the capturing force do cause him to be immediately executed by hanging; and I do further order that no commissioned officer of the United States taken captive shall be released on parole before exchange until the said Butler shall have met with due punishment for his crimes.

The order remained in effect until December 1862, when Butler was removed and replaced by Nathanial Banks. Banks repealed a number of

Jefferson Davis. *Courtesy*
Encyclopedia Virginia.

other orders issued by Butler, but that never eased the contempt that the people of New Orleans held for the Union troops.

Though the surrender of New Orleans was an easy victory for the Yankees, it was also a complicated one. By issuing his various orders, Butler made it increasingly difficult to run the city. However, Butler and Banks both realized that Union possession of New Orleans must be maintained at all costs. By controlling New Orleans, the Union was able to control all trade in the region south of the city. Controlling this area, coupled with the Union blockade in the Gulf of Mexico, not only gave the Federals a considerable amount of power but also paved the way for them to capture the Mississippi and complete Scott's Anaconda Plan.

Immediately after the Union captured New Orleans, a much smaller skirmish took place at the mouth of the Amite River on Lake Maurapas. The Amite River is roughly 117 miles long and runs by Baton Rouge, connecting it with Lake Maurapas. The river is a great backdoor to the city of New Orleans. If one must avoid the Mississippi River, especially during the Civil War and its age of the ironclads, then the Amite is the best route to take. The river flows south from Mississippi into Louisiana. To reach New

Orleans, one only has to take the river to Lake Maurapas, through Lake Pontchartrain and into the Crescent City.

On the morning of April 7, 1863, a Federal steamer, the USS *Barataria*, was on a reconnaissance mission. The USS *Barataria* was actually a Confederate ship that had been taken into custody by the Union army during the surrender of New Orleans. During a mission, the steamer became entangled. While entangled, the Federals were discovered attempting to free the steamer by a small group of Confederate guerrillas.

A skirmish ensued, and with the help of the Sixth Michigan, the commander of the *Barataria*, acting ensign James F. Perkins, was able to keep the determined Rebels at bay. While the Sixth Michigan was fighting off the Confederates, the ship's crew was busy trying to free the ship. Throughout the day, the crewmen tossed supplies and ammunition over the side of the steamer in an effort to lighten the load. The crew threw everything that was not nailed down overboard. They even went as far as to throw over the bow gun and empty the steamer's boiler.

Nevertheless, the ship remained stuck at the mouth of the Amite River. Realizing that there was nothing left to do, Perkins gave the order to scuttle the ship. Most of the crew abandoned ship and paddled ashore in small boats. A scuttling party remained behind to destroy the guns and set fire to the ship. The scuttling party was barely away from the *Barataria* when the flames reached what few stores of ammunition were left and exploded. The ship was a total loss. Though the Confederates did not take the ship, they definitely won the battle.

Chapter 7

Baton Rouge's First Brush with Blue and Troops on the Move

O nce New Orleans fell, the next stop on the Union path to capturing the Mississippi River was the capital city of Baton Rouge. Since Admiral David G. Farragut simply walked off his ship and claimed the Crescent City without any opposition—no gunshots or cannon fire—the Union decided to use this momentum to its favor.

In what will become known as the first Vicksburg Campaign, the Union fleet sailed north, up the Mississippi River, which was often referred to as the "inland sea," especially by General Sherman. The seven gunboats did not meet any real resistance as they sailed up the river, with the exception of random cannon fire as they passed Donaldsonville, Louisiana. As soon as New Orleans fell, the Confederate officials had the capital moved from Baton Rouge to Opelousas, and many of the locals followed suit. The citizens who did remain gazed upon the fleet with cold stares and great concerns. One of those locals was a young lady by the name of Eliza McHatton. Eliza and her husband, Alexander, lived on Arlington Plantation a few miles south of Baton Rouge. In her book, *From Flag to Flag*, she describes the scene and how she felt when the Union fleet arrived:

> *One magnificent morning in early summer the whole river, the silence on whose surface had remained now many weeks undisturbed, was suddenly, as if by magic, ablaze with the grandeur of Federal gunboats and transports with flags and bright-colored streamers flying from every peak, their decks thronged with brilliantly uniformed officers. We stood upon the veranda, with streaming eyes and bursting hearts.*

William Tecumseh Sherman. *www.archives.gov.*

Due to earlier flooding, there was a crevasse that opened up and separated Arlington from Baton Rouge. This breach in the levee prevented any communication between the two areas; therefore, any advance notice of the fleet's arrival was nearly impossible. Though this was not good news for the city, it did give McHatton some piece of mind. She goes on to write, "But the big gully at the mouth of the crevasse was still there, deep, muddy, and unutterably foul with the odor of dead fish lying stranded all about. The road was cut in two by an impassable barrier, a fathomless mud-hole. So the crevasse was a blessing…we were safe from unwelcome visitors." Shortly after the Federals arrived, the McHattons left the Baton Rouge area for Texas. They knew those unwelcome visitors were on their way.

Most of the fleet passed the capital city on their way to Vicksburg; however, the USS *Iroquois* dropped anchor on May 7, 1862. On the following day, its captain, James S. Palmer, demanded the city's surrender. In a note delivered to Mayor B.F. Bryan, the captain writes, "The same terms shall be

USS *Iroquois. Courtesy of United States Navy Historical Center.*

afforded the city of Baton Rouge as were granted to New Orleans; it must be surrendered to the naval forces of the United States." The note went on to state that rights and property of the citizens would remain in the locals' possession; however, any property belonging to the Confederate government would be turned over to the United States when demanded. Palmer also stated that the U.S. flag must be hoisted on the arsenal.

The mayor's reply was cordial yet stern: "The city of Baton Rouge will not be surrendered voluntarily to any power on Earth." As stern as this sounds, Bryan recognized the fact that the city had no real defense against the Union forces. Most of the soldiers were off protecting other Confederate interests throughout the region, the closest one being one of the most critical positions on the Mississippi River, Vicksburg. However, to the mayor it was the principle of the matter. Though there would be no battle, Federal position of Baton Rouge would "be without the consent and against the wish of the peaceable inhabitants." Consent or not, Palmer took possession of Baton Rouge the following day. He displayed this change of possession by hoisting the U.S. flag over the arsenal, just as he stated before. Nevertheless, the captain conveyed a harsh warning to the mayor: "This flag must remain unmolested, though I have no force on shore to protect it. The rash act of some individual may cause your city to pay a bitter penalty."

This warning fell on deaf ears. The *Iroquois* was called away to Vicksburg in an effort to take control of the town. Captain Lee of the U.S. Navy demanded the surrender of Vicksburg. Not only did Vicksburg refuse, but unlike Baton Rouge, the city had the means to defend itself. Nevertheless, in the Union troops' absence in Baton Rouge, a group of Rebels ripped down the newly hoisted American flag.

Captain James S. Palmer. *Courtesy of Library of Congress, Prints and Photographs Division.*

This episode was Baton Rouge's first brush with Federal troops. The interactions between the city and the Union soldiers were, for the most part, civil. In correspondence to his superiors, Palmer boasted how the mayor and other local authorities were courteous and "gentlemanlike." However, this civility quickly came to an end. The Union troops were only gone for several weeks. They returned to Baton Rouge on May 28, 1862. They were defeated at Vicksburg and retreated back to the former Louisiana capital to regroup and resupply. By this time, the stern politeness that had been written about in early correspondence had faded away and was replaced with bitter overzealousness.

On the return trip, a group of Union soldiers spotted a washwoman on the banks of the river. The group set out to proposition the woman to wash their laundry. However, before they could even reach the riverbank, they were fired upon by several Confederates positioned in shanties along the river. Three Union soldiers were wounded in the barrage. In retaliation, Admiral Farragut ordered the cannons to pummel the shanties. When the smoke cleared, it was discovered that the Rebel soldiers had escaped, and the only casualties were several women caught in the crossfire. This is only one example of how diplomacy quickly broke down between the blue and gray in Baton Rouge. Things would only prove to get worse as time went by.

Hearing word that the Union was on its way back to Baton Rouge, the few remaining residents did all they could to make the Federals' stay as inhospitable as possible. The locals knew that the troops would be starved for supplies and aid. Therefore, they began to destroy as many of these supplies as possible, especially cotton. Massive piles of cotton were burned in city squares. Barges loaded down with cotton were lit on fire and set adrift in the middle of the river. However, cotton was not the only commodity being destroyed. The Baton Rougeans also decided to make the city "dry" by destroying as much of the liquor as they could. The dumping of liquor became so prevalent that Sarah Morgan writes, "Gutters and pavements were filled with strong drinks."

General Williams returned to Baton Rouge with his men on May 29. Immediately, the Union took control of the ordnance depot, occupied the capitol and pitched tents on its grounds. After landing in Baton Rouge, Union troops seized the town. The entire town was a wash of blue uniforms from every rank. Upon their arrival, Union generals decided to lock down the port city.

Even though the people of Baton Rouge were in revolt, Williams had little trouble in occupying the city. This was largely due to the fact that when he arrived, Williams brought with him six regiments of infantry, two artillery batteries and a troop of cavalry.

However, in the process of locking down the city, it was also ransacked. Federal soldiers went door to door inspecting the area; it was during these inspections that many deserted homes were looted by Union soldiers. Whatever was not destroyed by the locals was being pillaged by the blue-clad servicemen. This type of behavior was not uncommon within the ranks of Union troops. When New Orleans fell, it was reported that the Union was looting the Crescent City and surrounding areas. This behavior disturbed Williams so much that he was compelled to write in his official report, "These regiments, officers and men, with rare exceptions, appear to be wholly destitute of the moral sense, and I believe that they believe, in the face of all remonstrances, exhortations, and disgust, expressed in no measured terms, that they regard pillaging not only a right in itself but a soldierly accomplishment."

There was more to the Union occupation of Baton Rouge than just looting. Williams ordered the construction of a variety of defenses placed in and around the city to protect their encampment. He also set up checkpoints along the major roads leading into Baton Rouge. The bustling port city was transformed. Shops and homes were replaced with earthen gun emplacements and stockades.

Even though there were no Confederate troops to be found in the city, it does not mean they were cowering in the swamps. The Confederates were making plans of their own. While Union troops were fortifying Baton Rouge, the Confederates were at Camp Moore planning a take-back of Baton Rouge.

Chapter 8

Skirmish on the Amite River and First Battle of Donaldsonville

At daybreak on July 24, 1862, a Federal force, led by Colonel McMillian, was traveling along the Amite River near present-day Denham Springs, Louisiana. As the men neared Benton's Ferry, they discovered a small company of Confederate rangers. The rangers, led by Captain Kemp, had nearly thirty horses and a variety of camp equipment in their possession. The Rebel rangers were on their way to meet a detachment of Wingfield's Partisan Rangers under the command of Captain Wilson. Wilson's men made camp four miles south of Curtis's Ferry. Seeking an opportunity to seize supplies and take the Rebels by surprise, McMillian called for an immediate attack. The Confederates were outnumbered and overwhelmed. After a short skirmish, Kemp ordered a full retreat.

While the small skirmish was taking place, Colonel McMillan sent a detachment of scouts to the camp near Curtis's Ferry. Once again, the Union troops took the Confederates by surprise. Another small skirmish ensued, and the Confederates were forced to retreat.

Donaldsonville, the county seat of Ascension Parish, was another strategic point on the Mississippi. Since the Union's arrival in the lower Mississippi, Confederate troops stationed in Donaldsonville did everything they could to slow their enemy's progress. From Donaldsonville, the Rebels would conduct sneak attacks on passing Union ships. The victims of the sneak attacks were mainly Union supply ships headed north. As the ships passed the town, they were commonly fired upon by Confederate artillery. Lieutenant Roe aboard the *Katadlin* vents his frustrations over the sneak attacks in his diary: "We are now constantly under fire of this covert kind as we pass up and down the river. Our fighting is a savage Indian warfare. The troops and guns are concealed and watch for us as we pass along the fire and flee. Sharp-shooters occupy the tree tops and take deliberate aim at our decks. We now regularly fight our way up and down the river."

There was little that General Benjamin F. Butler could do to stop them because his hands were full with the battle in Vicksburg and the securing of Baton Rouge. However, this situation quickly changed when the Union fell back from the First Battle at Vicksburg and their victory in the Battle of Baton Rouge. With these two issues temporarily resolved, Butler could focus his attention on the town that was causing him such problems.

It did not take long for Butler to redirect his attention. On August 9, 1862, only four days after the Union victory in Baton Rouge, General Butler ordered Admiral Farragut to dispatch a message to the mayor of Donaldsonville that read: "To the People of Donaldsonville, La: Every time my boats are fired upon I will burn a portion of your town. D.G. Farragut." Concerned that this declaration was no idle threat, the mayor of Donaldsonville called an emergency meeting with several Confederate officials in the area. They agreed to meet in the town of Thibodaux, along Bayou Lafourche. Thibodaux was the county seat of Lafourche Parish and, at that time, was free from Union control. However, this lack of Union presence changed by October 1862.

The meeting took place at the end of July 1862. In attendance were the mayor, General Mouton, Captain James McWaters and Governor Thomas Moore. The mayor was prepared to comply with Farragut's request; however, the others were not. Though it is unclear what exactly was said during the meeting, the consensus was that as long as the Union persisted to sail the Mississippi, the Confederacy would continue to fire upon its vessels. It has been reported that a major contributing factor in making that decision was the fact that Donaldsonville was home to a convent and an

General Alfred Mouton.

orphanage. The Rebels were betting that Farragut would not have the audacity to fire on a town that harbored nuns and defenseless children. This was a gamble that did not pay off.

After hearing that city officials were refusing to comply with his request, Farragut sent a small party of soldiers ashore, not to attack the town but to deliver one final message—evacuate. The admiral gave the citizens three days to pack their belongings and clear out of town. This time, most of the locals complied with his request. Interestingly, the nuns did not evacuate themselves or the children. Instead they chose to ride out the pending attack within the walls of the convent. Nevertheless, Admiral Farragut ordered the shelling to begin right on cue.

The Federals shelled the town for hours, leveling most of it. The riverfront was reduced to rubble. In an odd twist of fate, the convent and the orphanage survived the barrage with only minor damage. Though severely shaken, neither the convent nor the orphanage sustained any casualties. Unfortunately for the town, the shelling was only the first wave of the attack. Once the bombardment ended, Farragut sent a tremendous landing party ashore to finish what the artillery had started. Within minutes of the party landing on the banks of the Mississippi River, the Donaldsonville riverfront was set ablaze.

To this day, it remains unclear how the convent and orphanage survived the attack unscathed. In response to a letter written by Mother Superior scolding General Butler, his admiral and his troops for putting the lives of the innocent and defenseless in such peril, Butler explains, "Any injury must have been entirely accidental." In his apology, Butler did not specify why this was entirely accidental. There is no evidence that Butler or Farragut ever gave an explicit order to spare the convent or the orphanage.

Even though the convent and orphanage were spared, the rest of Donaldsonville was in ruins. The devastation proved to the locals that Admiral Farragut did not make it a habit to make idle threats. Two days after the destruction of Donaldsonville, local officials met and signed a cease and desist order. With this order, Union troops occupied Donaldsonville, using it as a base of operations for a wide variety of skirmishes up and down Bayou Lafourche, including the larger Battle of Labadieville. However, this was not the last time that the city of Donaldsonville would see bloodshed and destruction.

Chapter 9

The Rebels Plan to Take Back Baton Rouge and the Federals Dig in Their Heels

With the Federals back in Baton Rouge, the generals of the Confederacy were making plans to take back the capital city. Needing to regroup themselves, Confederate troops pulled back to Camp Moore. This new base of operations was about seventy miles from Baton Rouge, putting plenty of space between themselves and the Union.

Named after Governor Thomas Overton Moore, the camp was responsible for assembling, organizing and training many of the Confederate soldiers dispatched across the South. The camp was established long before the fall of Baton Rouge and was chosen because of its access to the New Orleans, Jackson and Great Northern Railroad, which is known as the Illinois Central Railroad today. Such access was of great benefit to the Confederacy. At the start of the Civil War, this railroad was considered to be one of the best in the South. It boasted seven locomotives and eleven passenger cars with the capability to handle any increase in traffic.

Aside from the easy access to the railroad, the geography of the area made the camp well suited for a base of operations. Due to its position between Beaver Creek and the Tangipahoa River, there was an abundance of fresh drinking water to supply the troops. These tributaries also allowed men and supplies to be transported by boat instead of relying entirely on the railroad. The climate at Camp Moore was also much more bearable than at most other Confederate camps in Louisiana. Many of the soldiers often wrote home about the pleasant climate in Camp Moore, especially about how it seemed that the camp had far fewer mosquitoes than any other camp in the state.

Above: Camp Moore.

Left: John C. Breckinridge. *Courtesy of Library of Congress, Prints and Photographs Division.*

General John C. Breckinridge arrived at the camp on July 28, 1862. In his command were the Louisiana, Tennessee, Arkansas, Mississippi and Kentucky units, composed of nearly four thousand men. Breckinridge combined his men with those of General Daniel Ruggles. Ruggles, who had at least one thousand men under his command, was West Point trained and led a division of men during the Battle of Shiloh. Also at Camp Moore during Breckinridge's regrouping was General Charles Clark, who was a veteran of the Battle of Shiloh as well. While leading his division, Clark was wounded in the shoulder; however, that did not stop him from joining Breckinridge's plan in ousting the Federals from Baton Rouge.

With the additional men, Breckinridge was able to create two separate divisions, one led by Ruggles and the other led by Clark. Breckinridge also called in the cavalry. Known as the Partisan Rangers, these mounted guerrillas were dispatched to act as pickets along the Amite River. This guerrilla force was composed of about 837 men experienced in picket duty in and around the area. Though Ruggles was not particularly fond of the Partisan Rangers, he turned a blind eye to their presence and focused on leading his division. Part of his division included the First Louisiana Battery.

The First Louisiana Battery was led by Captain Oliver J. Semmes and consisted of two rifled six-pound cannons and four smoothbore six-pound cannons. Ruggles's plan was to use the artillery just as he had used it at Shiloh. His plan was to amass the guns at the center of the line instead of breaking them up among the various regiments. Ruggles was the first to use artillery in this manner. This technique proved so effective that it became a common use of artillery during the latter part of the war.

However, if he was to successfully remove the Federals from Baton Rouge, Breckingridge knew he needed one more component in place. Baton Rouge's proximity to the Mississippi River provided the Union with a strong naval presence in the area. As long as that naval presence persisted, Breckinridge knew he did not have a chance in winning back the capital city. He needed

General Daniel Ruggles. *Courtesy of Library of Congress, Prints and Photographs Division.*

some way to incapacitate the Federal navy so his troops could get close to the riverfront, ultimately liberating Baton Rouge from Union control. His solution to the Federal navy was the CSS *Arkansas*.

The ironclad warship was a maritime marvel of its time. It combined a metal-skinned hull, steam propulsion and a main armament of guns that fired exploding shells. It was a warship that the Federals feared. The Union navy had every right to fear this ship. The *Arkansas* could run at eight knots carrying 232 men, along with its ten guns. Those guns included two 8-inch Columbiads in the bow ports and two 6.4-inch Brooke rifles in the stern ports. The broadside ports were home to two 6.4-inch Brooke rifles, two 8-inch Dahlgren smoothbores and two thirty-two-pound smoothbores. This deadly package was wrapped in railroad iron over wood, with the exception of the stern. This portion of the ship was covered entirely with boiler iron. To make this ship even more menacing, a cast-iron ram was located at the bow of the ship in case of close combat.

With all of these weapons at its disposal, the *Arkansas* proved to be a formidable opponent for the Union. During the first Battle of Vicksburg, the ironclad was credited with twenty-three kills and wounding fifty-nine others while only sustaining minimal damage and casualties. However, the *Arkansas*' success in Vicksburg is also attributed to its captain, Issac N. Brown. Due to his actions in Vicksburg, Brown was promoted to commander in August 1862. However, after the daring run in Vicksburg, the CSS *Arkansas* was due for some much-needed repairs. While the ship was in for repairs, Brown

CSS *Arkansas. Courtesy of U.S. Naval Historical Center Navy Art Collection.*

requested and was granted four days' leave. In Brown's absence, the *Arkansas* was left in the command of Lieutenant Henry Stevens, but Breckinridge needed a naval presence for his march on Baton Rouge. Therefore, when he telegraphed General Van Dorn to request the assistance of the *Arkansas*, Van Dorn (knowing the important of the Baton Rouge plan) obliged. This would prove to be a disastrous decision since the ironclad was not fully repaired, nor did it have its captain. Nevertheless, the CSS *Arkansas* was dispatched from Vicksburg to Baton Rouge.

With this final, and key, component in place, Breckinridge had his plan to take back Baton Rouge. With the troops ready, the Partisan Rangers on picket duty and the *Arkansas* on its way, Breckinridge planned to liberate Baton Rouge from Union control on August 5, 1862.

The spark of Confederate energy did not go unnoticed. The sudden movement of troops and supplies, as subtle as it was, grabbed the attention of General Williams. If it was not the Confederate movement that the Federals noticed, it was most certainly the movement of the locals. Concluding that these were signs of a Rebel attack, Williams made preparations.

These preparations included further fortifying the capital city. The Federal general ordered his men to dig entrenchments around the arsenal, along with strengthening pickets and outposts. While the defenses were being reinforced, Williams took the opportunity to begin placing his troops in key positions around the city. Just as Breckinridge knew that this battle would entail two major components, land and naval, Williams was well aware that he would need the combined efforts of the Federal army and navy to keep Baton Rouge in the Union's possession. Williams started by positioning his men in a wide arc on the eastern side of the city.

He placed artillery emplacements along with the Fourth and Ninth Wisconsin Regiments near the site of the present-day Governor's Mansion, which was not constructed until 1963. The Fourteenth Maine Regiment was positioned on North Street in an area presently known as the Spanish Town Historic District. Williams placed another artillery regiment, the Sixth Massachusetts Light Artillery, in the center of his citywide arc. The Sixth Massachusetts was equipped with four twelve-pound Napoleons. These smoothbore cannons were popular throughout the Civil War and were admired for their killing power at close range. The Twenty-first Indiana Regiment, also known as the Jackass Regiment, was positioned near North Nineteenth Street, near the location of the Baton Rouge National Cemetery. At the end of the arc was the Sixth Michigan Regiment, which was located near present-day City Park.

TOPOGRAPHICAL PLAN
OF THE CITY
AND
BATTLE-FIELD
OF
BATON·ROUGE, LA.
Fought on the 5th of August
1862
drawn by
JOSEPH GORLINSKI, Civil Eng.
Scale of feet

From a map on file in the office of the Chief of Engineers, U.S. Army

Map of the Battle of Baton Rouge, 1862.

The second factor in Williams's defense of Baton Rouge was naval. To protect the captured city, he had the full force of a Union armada behind him. This armada boasted eighty guns, including the impressive one-hundred-pound Parrott rifle that was aboard the USS *Westfield*. Accompanying the

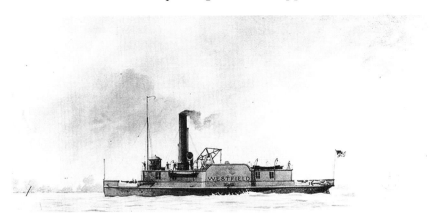

USS *Westfield. Courtesy of Naval History and Heritage Command.*

Westfield were ten other ships: two sloops of war, two steam gunboats, four Unadilla-class gunboats, a light-draft side-wheel gunboat and their very own ironclad, the USS *Essex*. Aside from the sheer number of guns on the river, the river itself was on the side of the Union. The river was still running high, which provided the gunboats a much better trajectory and much better line of sight on the streets of the capital city. With his men and boats in place, Williams was prepared for a Rebel march on Baton Rouge. Unfortunately for Williams, the Union general was not sure when this impending attack was coming or exactly how he was going to defend his stolen city.

Chapter 10
Breckinridge's March

Breckinridge mobilized his troops. The first division, led by General Clark, left early so they could secure William's Bridge on the Amite River. This bridge was the easiest point on the Amite River to cross. Once the bridge was secure, Breckinridge sent the second division, led by General Ruggles, to rendezvous with Clark and his men two days later.

It is still unclear why Breckinridge sent Clark and his men in advance to secure William's Bridge. Though it is a strategic position on the Amite River, the Partisan Rangers were sent out to establish pickets at various locations along the Amite River. It is possible that Daniel Ruggles's disdain for the rangers could have rubbed off on Breckinridge, or it simply could have been easier and more efficient to move the Confederate force in two separate divisions. Even though the terrain was easy to cross, the sheer distance the soldiers had to travel was extensive. One soldier described the route as an "interminable pine forest." The long trek from Camp Moore was slow, tedious and largely uneventful for both divisions. Clark and his men arrived on schedule. Just as planned, Ruggles and his men joined Clark on August 2, 1862. The two divisions made camp on the bank of the Amite River before moving on to the Comite River. This next trek through southeast Louisiana would take Breckinridge and his army south down Greenwell Springs Road.

The Greenwell Springs area has an interesting history of its own. The area can trace its modern origins to the 1850s, when Robert W. Greenwell purchased a large plot of land to develop a resort hotel near the present-day Greenwell Springs Hospital. The reason Greenwell chose this particular site is due to the fact that it contained ten naturally flowing springs, which

Charles Clark.

Greenwell claimed to have medicinal properties. It was said that each spring could cure a different ailment. He named his resort the Greenwell Springs Hotel. During the nineteenth century, it was common for the wealthy residents of metropolitan areas to leave their city dwellings during the hot summer months for more hospitable climates. During the summer, cities were often plagued with diseases such as malaria or, at the very least, reeked due to the poor sanitation in urban areas of the nineteenth century. Even though Robert Greenwell did not fight in the Battle of Baton Rouge, his hotel plays an important role in its aftermath. As for Greenwell himself, he did eventually join the Confederate cause. He was a captain and commanded Company F, Third Louisiana Calvary, during the Siege of Port Hudson. Greenwell Springs Road ran through this resort area, but in 1862, it was nothing more than a narrow, dusty road that left limited room for the Confederates to travel on.

Breckinridge and his two divisions made it to the Comite River Bridge on August 4, 1862. This bridge was only ten miles outside the capital city. With less than twenty-four hours before the start of the attack, the Confederates made camp on the banks of the Comite River. This had to be a much-needed break for the Rebels. The soldiers had traveled nearly sixty miles to their Comite campsite from Camp Moore. Not only were they physically exhausted, but they were mentally exhausted as well. In an attempt to keep morale high, Breckinridge gave a speech to his men in which he implied that the battle would be quickly and easily won. The men trusted their general, and when they heard him promise an easy win, morale increased nearly tenfold. However, in a matter of hours, Breckinridge would receive news that would not only break his spirit but ultimately force him to break his promise of an easy win.

To maintain their schedule, the Confederates broke camp and left the Comite River later that night. During the early morning hours of August 5, Breckinridge made it to Ward's Creek, which was located about one mile east of the present-day Magnolia Cemetery. As his men were getting into place, Breckinridge received word that the ironclad CSS *Arkansas*, on which the Confederate win depended, was on schedule. The *Arkansas* was several miles upriver, passing the port city of Bayou Sara. With this news, the Confederate general was confident that his plan to reclaim Baton Rouge would start as planned. What will become known as the Battle of Baton Rouge would commence at dawn on August 5, 1862.

Unbeknownst to the Confederates, the CSS *Arkansas* was on schedule, but barely. From the very beginning of the trek to Baton Rouge, the ironclad was plagued with problems. The crew was forced to stop several times before reaching Bayou Sara to make engine repairs. To add insult to injury, the ship was running without its usual captain or engineer. The entire battle hinged on the participation of the Arkansas. For Breckinridge's plan to work, the ironclad had to be there to keep the Federal navy busy. Without it, there was no way for Breckinridge to make it to the riverbank because of the bombardment from the Union armada. Without the ironclad, the Confederates would surely lose the battle.

Chapter 11

The Confederates Open the Ball in Baton Rouge

Breckinridge marched down Main Street with Clark's division on his right and Ruggles's division on his left. The sudden movement of Confederate soldiers spooked the local wildlife. Just as many of the local Baton Rougeans fled the city when they heard a battle was coming, the wildlife fled the woods as the army marched forward. However, the march toward Federally controlled Baton Rouge pushed the scared animals through the Union camp. This sudden movement of wildlife, along with the sound of gunfire off in the distance, confirmed Williams's notion that the Confederates would try to retake Baton Rouge.

The premature gunshots that alerted Williams to oncoming Confederates were due to a small party of Partisan Rangers. It seems that the small party was advancing too quickly under the orders of Major James De Baun. Instead of stopping at Ward's Creek, as ordered, the rangers continued down Greenwell Springs Road. The party advanced until they happened upon a picket of the Twenty-first Indiana. The Union troops fired a volley in the direction of the rangers.

Under the orders of Captain Tate, the party retreated to relay the newly found intelligence back to the Confederate command. The small group of Partisan Rangers reached Brigadier General Benjamin H. Helm's Orphan Brigade. However, the old saying "It's darkest before the dawn" must be true, because in the morning darkness, which was compounded by the setting of fog over the area, Helm's brigade mistook the rangers for Union cavalry and began to fire into the darkness. As Helm's brigade mistakenly fired on their allies, the Partisan Rangers, in turn, mistook Helm's brigade for another Union picket.

Benjamin H. Helm.

The dual cases of mistaken identity resulted in an exchange of fire, but the mistake was soon realized, and a cease-fire was called. Unfortunately, the damage was done. During the barrage, the Partisan Rangers lost several men and horses either to death or injuries. Helm's brigade suffered even more: the brigade lost Helm himself. The brigadier general was badly wounded when his horse fell on top of him. He would eventually recover from those wounds, but for the Battle of Baton Rouge, Helm was replaced by Colonel Thomas H. Hunt. On top of losing their general, they also lost two out of three guns when they were made unserviceable by teams that bolted and overturned the pieces. Another young soldier—Lieutenant Alexander H. Todd, brother of Mary Todd Lincoln and brother-in-law to Abraham Lincoln—was killed in the exchange.

The battle would last the greater part of the morning. Starting at first light, the Confederates began the battle with a jump on the Union; however, with a dense fog rolling in, it was difficult for the Rebels to stay in formation. Overall, the fog wreaked havoc and created chaos for both armies. The Union armada was sitting blind on the Mississippi. Visibility was near zero, but tensions were high. At any moment, Union crews waited for the CSS *Arkansas* to burst out of the fog and ram into them. The Union was not yet aware, just like the Confederates, that the CSS *Arkansas* was not going to burst out of the fog.

All morning long, the Confederates were able to drive back each Union unit they encountered. It seemed that the Confederates had the forward momentum to take back Baton Rouge. With the Rebels on their heels, the Union was forced to fall back to a defensive position closer to the river. In this position, the Union had protection of the Federal armada. The Union gunboats on the river immediately began shelling the Confederates.

During the retreat, Union commander brigadier general Thomas Williams was killed, and the new commander, Colonel Thomas W. Cahill, replaced him. Under the lead of Cahill and the protection of the gunboats, the Union army was able to hold its position. The Union fleet had been waiting in anticipation for the opportunity to contribute to the battle. The *Essex* and the *Sumter* were located above the city and had clear fields of fire over the Bayou Gross. Both ships opened on the Confederate left flank, but it was the powerful eleven-inch guns of the *Essex* that caused the most damage to the Confederate line. The three smooth "soda bottle"–shaped Dahlgren guns hammered away at the Confederate line on the left. As soon as it was safe enough to fire, the USS *Kineo* and the USS *Katahdin* opened fire on the right. The combined barrage of the four ships decimated the Confederate ranks. Even with the *Kineo* and *Katahdin* firing their guns over the city, the shells were hitting their Confederate targets. Nevertheless, Breckinridge held the line. He knew that if his army was going to reclaim Baton Rouge, he needed the CSS *Arkansas* to neutralize the Union gunboats. The general was confident that all he needed to do was hold the line and wait.

It was his heavy reliance on the *Arkansas'* participation that was a major flaw in Breckinridge's plan. The Rebel ironclad would never make it to Baton Rouge. About ten miles north of Baton Rouge, the crew of the ironclad caught sight of their Federal adversaries. Just at that moment, the starboard engine of the battered and overworked ironclad failed. This failure caused the *Arkansas* to veer right, effectively tangling the gunboat in a series of submerged tree stumps along the river's banks. The crew could do nothing but listen to the sounds of the battle as the engineers rushed to repair Breckinridge's only hope. As luck would have it, the Union fleet was in the midst of shelling the city and did not notice the crippled ship. It took the greater part of the day to get the ship repaired and free from the riverbank.

Though under constant fire, Breckinridge and his men were hopeful of the *Arkansas'* arrival and were maintaining their position through the afternoon. However, upon the arrival of a messenger, all hope was lost. Without the *Arkansas*, Breckinridge had little hope in winning this battle. He writes, "The enemy had several batteries commanding the approaches to the arsenal and barracks and the gunboats had already reopened upon us with a direct fire. Under the circumstances, although the troops showed the utmost indifference to danger and death, and were reluctant to retire, I did not deem it prudent to pursue the victory further."

Chapter 12

The Fall of the CSS *Arkansas*

E ven though the battle was over, the *Arkansas'* troubles had only begun. Once freed, Lieutenant Henry K. Stevens decided that going into Baton Rouge would serve no purpose other than to get his crew killed. Therefore, Stevens ordered his crew upstream in order to put on coal and test the patched-up engines. After barely moving a quarter-mile upriver, the pin snapped on the starboard connecting rod. Once again, the *Arkansas* was forced to undergo repairs on the bank of the Mississippi. Still wary of the Union fleet just downriver, the crews worked as fast as they could, but repairing the ship took all night. Repairs were completed on the morning of August 6, but none of the crew was confident that the engines would last. Furthermore, Stevens just took sight of the USS *Essex*, and it was closing in fast. With no other options, Brown ordered his men to prepare for a fight. As the Rebel ironclad moved into position, its engines failed once more—a failure from which the CSS *Arkansas* would never recover.

Almost simultaneously, the pin snapped on the port connecting rod and the starboard engine simply stopped working. The CSS *Arkansas* was dead in the water. The *Essex* fired on the *Arkansas*, and though the crew attempted to return fire, it was quickly realized that the *Essex* was out of range of the Rebel ironclad's guns. The *Arkansas* drifted to the riverbank once more, and Stevens made the decision to scuttle the ship. He ordered his men off the once-feared ironclad, leaving a small scuttling party to destroy the ship. The scuttling party loaded the guns and set the ship ablaze. To mark the end of its military career, the CSS *Arkansas* exploded and vanished into the Mississippi River.

Sinking of the
CSS *Arkansas*.
*Courtesy of Naval
History and
Heritage Command.*

To avoid Union capture, Stevens ordered his men inland. The lieutenant described the retreat: "We travelled through Louisiana partly on foot, horseback, and in wagons, the planters and their wives and daughters receiving us all along our route with utmost kindness." Stevens and his men made it to Camp Moore. Shortly after arriving, the sailors left the camp by train for Jackson, Mississippi.

With Baton Rouge lost, Breckinridge had no choice but to retreat as well. He ordered his men to fall back while the Kentucky Seventh and Semmes Battery covered the retreating Rebels. The Confederates fell back to the Greenwell Springs Hotel, where the soldiers could find fresh water and assess their losses. The battle took a toll on the Confederate army. The battle had cost Breckinridge roughly 84 killed, 315 wounded and 57 missing. The Union did not fare much better. Its losses are estimated to be about 84 killed, 266 wounded and 33 missing.

Meanwhile, Van Dorn sent Bowen's Brigade from Vicksburg along with the Twelfth Louisiana to Breckinridge. His orders were clear: with the aid of the brigade, Breckinridge was to take the remainder of his troops to Port Hudson to fortify the area. While the Confederates made their way to Port Hudson, the Union forces laid waste to the city of Baton Rouge.

Fearing another attempt by the Confederates to retake the city, Colonel Halbert Paine, who was placed in charge after Williams's death, ordered the destruction of about one-third of the town to clear a line of sight for the gunboats on the river. Paine did not want to rely on signalmen, as had his predecessor. What was left of the town was looted continuously for a week. All of a sudden, Butler had a change of heart. Whether he realized that

Baton Rouge was not as strategic a post as he once thought or because of his men's lack of discipline or due to the Confederate surge into Port Hudson, Butler ordered his men to evacuate Baton Rouge back to New Orleans—but not before ordering the entire city burned to the ground. General Godfrey Weitzel, an engineer, pointed out the orphanage and insane asylum and convinced Butler to rescind the order. Instead of burning the city, Butler had every remaining resource stripped from it.

Among the Union evacuation was the Sixth Massachusetts Light Artillery, which was headed to Carrollton. A chaplain of the regiment, describing the damage of war-torn Baton Rouge, said, "The town, what there is left of it, is a deserted, desolate place. The streets are forsaken, the stores are closed. To the east of us are a large number of stacks of chimneys which are all that is left of what six months ago were elegant residences."

The Civil War left its mark on Baton Rouge. The city would never be the same again. Though the Confederates lost the battle, the Union did not really gain anything from it. They did, of course, keep the city of Baton Rouge under Union control, which brought them one step closer to gaining control of the Mississippi River. Yet the reality of it all was that Baton Rouge offered no real strategic gains. Moreover, the city was actually more of a liability, being that it was not easily defendable. It took a large amount of resources and effort to defend a city that offered so little. It seems that the Battle of Baton Rouge was more a battle of principle—basically, a show of force. The Union used the battle to show the Rebels that the city would remain under Federal control, while the Confederates set out to prove that they were able to take back and defend what was rightfully theirs.

Both sides, Union and Confederate, seemed to have depleted their resources only to have to face each other again for one of the most strategic points on the Mississippi River—Port Hudson. Only a few miles upriver, the tiny town of Port Hudson was a much more strategic location than the city of Baton Rouge. It was situated on the first high ground north of Baton Rouge and overlooked a severe bend in the river, a deadly obstacle for Union warships. Both sides needed Port Hudson to control the river from Baton Rouge to Vicksburg. Those Confederate soldiers who survived the Battle of Baton Rouge were sent to help fortify the city against a Union attack. In an attempt to take Port Hudson, the Union was in the process of sending nearly forty thousand men. These preparations, on the part of both the North and the South, laid the foundation for some of the bloodiest battles in the Civil War. Nearly nine months after the Battle of Baton Rouge, the blue and gray would be pitted against each other in what would become the most enduring and difficult siege of the Civil War.

Chapter 13

Bayou Sara

E ven though Bayou Sara never really saw any major battles, the once growing port city was home to some unusual occurrences during the Civil War. The town, now incorporated into the town of St. Francisville, was nestled at the foot of the bluffs that looked down onto the Mississippi River. Perched on those bluffs was Bayou Sara's sister city, St. Francisville. Because of its location, the town became a bustling port city and a major depot for goods between New Orleans and Natchez, Mississippi. Just prior to the Civil War, a journalist from New Orleans, J.W. Dorr, visited the area and described it as follows:

> *If St. Francisville is stronger on the ornamental, Bayou Sara is out of sight ahead of her on the practical, for she does all the business and a great deal of business is done, too. It is a thriving and bustling place, and contains some of the most extensive and heavily stocked stores in Louisiana, outside of New Orleans and there are few in New Orleans even which can surpass in value of stock the concern of Meyers, Hoffman and Co., dry goods dealers and direct importers.*

However, Meyers, Hoffman and Co. was not the only business in the area. Bayou Sara possessed all manners of goods and services to its local patron, including restaurants, saloons and hotels, the most notable being the China Grove Hotel. Even though the town itself was described as plain and utilitarian, Bayou Sara did have one building to note—Robinson Mumford's Bank of Exchange and Deposit. This building impressed Dorr the most:

"A prominent object in the town, occupying a very handsome building is Robinson Mumford's Bank of Exchange and Deposit."

Bayou Sara was on its way to becoming a major city on the banks of the Mississippi River. However, even before the Civil War began, the up-and-coming town ran into several hardships. One of these was when a fire broke out, burning nearly half the town. The town was no stranger to major fires, but this particular fire destroyed the main portion of town. Bayou Sara was in the midst of rebuilding and recovering from the fire when the Civil War began. This marked the beginning of a steady plague of incidents, affairs and skirmishes from which the town would never fully recover.

The first of these incidents occurred on the afternoon of August 10, 1862. According to reports, the USS *Essex* anchored just off the riverbank near Bayou Sara around four o'clock. Initially, it was there to replenish its coal supply. About an hour later, a transport sailed upriver. Upon the transport's arrival, the *Essex* began shelling the shore, predominantly at the road near the ferry landing. Under the protection of the *Essex*, the transport docked at the ferry landing. Brigadier General C.Y. Rowley of the Louisiana Militia described what followed next in his report:

USS *Essex*. *Courtesy of Naval History and Heritage Command.*

The transport then came to the ferry, landing on this side, and took on board a quantity of sugar lying there to be carried across to Bayou Sara. They compelled the Negroes of Bemis and Col. Stephen Van Wickle to roll the sugar on board, while 100-armed men stood guard over them. They notified Mr. Gill to have his hands ready to put another lot on board which was lying three-quarters of a mile above, but they left this side before it was accomplished, the whole or larger part being on this bank this morning.

Rowley also suspected that the Union pirates pillaged another large quantity of sugar from the railroad depot, but he could neither confirm nor deny if it was aboard the ironclad.

The townspeople and the Confederates could do nothing except watch as the sugar was stolen. Most of the Confederate forces were elsewhere. The closest company was fifteen miles south of Bayou Sara. The second closest was Captain Thompson's rangers forty-five miles away and across the river near the Atchafalaya Basin. Knowing his hands were tied, Rowley's distress is easily inferred in his report when he states, "We could do nothing to prevent these marauders from executing their plans."

The brigadier general immediately sent a message to the surrounding troops to bring them back to town to prevent a similar attack. Also, Colonel F.H. Farrar had guards stationed on every road throughout the night in an effort to capture any "stragglers" and prevent any slave, or anyone else for that matter, from meeting with Union soldiers.

At the time, it was unclear to the general whether this was an isolated incident of pillaging or if Bayou Sara was another target in the Union's effort to capture the Mississippi. Nevertheless, the incident was a small victory for the Union. It is estimated that the Union transport sailed away with four to five hundred hogsheads of sugar that belonged to speculators. They also took aboard two or three people who were known to be "engaged in crossing sugar" as prisoner.

The Confederates were not going to take this attack lying down. On August 15, they found their chance to retaliate. The USS *Sumter* grounded near Bayou Sara. Though the captain and its crew tried to free the ship, they were unsuccessful and decided to sail downriver in a yawl to acquire some assistance.

The *Sumter* was a 525-ton side-wheel steamer that carried four thirty-two-pounders and one twelve-pounder gun. The steamer started its career as a towboat but was purchased by the Confederates in 1861. Under the Confederate flag, the steamer was renamed the CSS *General Sumter* and refitted as a cotton-clad ram. In addition to covering the bow with four-inch oak sheathing covered by one-inch iron plates, the Confederates also compressed cotton bales between double pine bulkheads for added strength. It operated under the Confederate flag until June 1862, when it ran aground and was captured by the Union navy during the Battle of Memphis. The Union repaired and renamed the steamer the USS *Sumter*.

Now grounded again near Bayou Sara, the Confederates took their chance. A small force of troops attacked the grounded ship, boarded it and stripped it of anything they could carry. *Harper's New Monthly Magazine*, in February 1863, reported, "The *Essex* hastily returned to that place on the 16th, but too late to prevent the destruction of the *Sumter*, which had been fired by the citizens. They had also, contrary to agreement, shot at and wounded Union men residing there, and grossly maltreated all politically opposed to them, of whatever sex. The stores also which the *Sumter* had been left to protect had been destroyed."

Though a small victory for the Confederates, in the long run, it would cause more trouble for Bayou Sara. Upon hearing the news of the *Sumter*, Union forces were planning on making sure that no other attacks on Union vessels would occur. A Union correspondent wrote, "Capt. PORTER, of the *Essex*, has since started up the river with a determination to demolish any place along the banks which has been used as to protect guerrilla bands engaged in firing upon our steamboats and other National craft."

Barely two weeks later, the *Essex* and its Union troops returned to Bayou Sara. The actual reason behind the Union's return is still unclear, but a reasonable guess would be that they were in search of coal. It may have been another pillaging expedition or just another mission to slow or stop the flow of supplies into the Confederate interior. Nevertheless, on August 25, 1862, the *Essex* returned to Bayou Sara and once again began shelling the town. The shelling did not really do much damage to the town. However, it did provide cover for the two boatloads of Union soldiers as they landed on the riverbank. It was these soldiers who caused the most damage in the town. As soon as they landed, they began to set fire to the town. A dispatch to the *Grenada Appeal* stated, "All the houses on the levee were burned except two." Those that did not burn were pillaged, stripped of anything that was valuable and of any use.

The entire affair did not last long. As soon as they pillaged the unburned homes, the Union soldiers were back onto their boats and steaming downriver. The few Confederate troops that were stationed at Bayou Sara did fire upon the Union pirates, which is probably why they focused their efforts on the riverfront. On the riverfront, the Union troops had the protection of the *Essex*'s guns. *Harper's New Monthly Magazine* reported:

> *A heavy musketry fire was poured on the officers and men from the* Essex *as they advanced toward the center of the town from the buildings which were turned into places of concealment, compelling the boat's crew to retreat toward the shore under cover of the guns of their vessel which opened on the enemy with shell, and soon led to the abandonment of their position.*

All in all, nothing was gained from the skirmish. The *Essex* and its men were in search of coal, most of which was set fire and destroyed by the Confederates to keep it out of the hands of their adversaries. Yet by this time, it does seem that most of the civilians had fled the river town and most of the inhabitants still there were Confederate troops.

Chapter 14

The USS *Essex* Arrives at Port Hudson

On September 7, 1862, Port Hudson received its first taste of a Union assault. This was a small naval assault that consisted of the USS *Essex* and the USS *Anglo-American*. The *Essex* and the *Anglo-American* were traveling downriver to Federally occupied New Orleans. Sources disagree on who fired the first shot. While some contend that Commander David Dixon Porter ordered the assault on Port Hudson, there are others who believe that the *Essex* was fired upon by the shore batteries at Port Hudson. Nevertheless, the Union ironclad that was instrumental in the Federal victory at Baton Rouge was now knocking on Port Hudson's door.

The Confederate batteries consisted of the salvaged guns from the recently destroyed CSS *Arkansas*. Much of the crew was from the destroyed Rebel ironclad, as well. The Confederates were in the process of fortifying Port Hudson. Since the loss of Baton Rouge, the Union was getting uncomfortably close to gaining control of the Mississippi River. Port Hudson was the last line of defense south of Vicksburg. By September 1862, the Union controlled most of the Mississippi south of Baton Rouge. They were constantly engaged in campaigns in the Teche region of the state and were looking to seize control of the Mississippi River at the mouth of the Red River.

The assault did not last long. The two sides exchanged fire for a short period of time, and then the Yankees called off the attack and sailed back to New Orleans. The *Essex* seems to have sustained most of the damage. It was reported that the ironclad suffered at least fourteen hits. On the other hand, Port Hudson sustained very little damage in the assault, but the

Coaling Farragut's fleet. *Courtesy of Library of Congress.*

Confederates learned that their efforts to fortify the position were not made in vain. Though small, Port Hudson easily withstood the Union attack.

Even though Port Hudson passed its first test with flying colors, the Confederates had a lot more work ahead of them. The Union would certainly return, and when they did, they would have more men, more guns and more boats at their disposal. Also, when the Union returned, the task to bring down Port Hudson would not be left to Porter. The Union would entrust that task to the formidable Nathanial P. Banks.

Chapter 15

The Battle of Labadieville

I n Assumption Parish, near the town of Labadieville, the Confederates were forced to make a stand in a small skirmish on October 27, 1862. General Mouton was nearly outflanked by Brigadier General Godfrey Weitzel. Weitzel was in the region to attempt to redirect the resources, such as sugar and cotton, that traveled up Bayou Lafourche from the southern parishes into Union possession. Two days prior to the skirmish, Weitzel had arrived in Donaldsonville and begun his march south, down on the east bank of the bayou, with about four thousand men. A regimental historian with the Thirteenth Connecticut described the march:

> *We passed several villages, and saw two camps, just vacated, the fires still blazing. One of these was so well built, with comfortable cane-roofed huts. These quickly disappeared in smoke, the burning stalks bursting with loud explosions, which rattled like pistol firing. At several points we saw hastily-constructed breastworks and rifle-pits, which the enemy abandoned without contest. Great numbers of negroes left their owners' plantations and joined us, bringing with them mules, turkeys, furniture, and bundles of clothing.*

To avoid this Yankee maneuver, Mouton ordered the Eighteenth Louisiana and the Crescent Regiment to take a position on the west bank, near Georgia Landing. Meanwhile, he ordered the Thirty-third Louisiana and Terrebonne Regiments to hold the east bank. With the completion of these orders, Mouton now had several hundred cavalrymen and a battery on either side of the bayou, and the Union army was quickly approaching.

Godfrey Weitzel. *Courtesy of Library of Congress, Prints and Photographs Division.*

On the morning of October 27, the two forces clashed about one mile north of Labadieville. Ralston's battery, on the west bank, was able to keep the Union army at bay for a short time. Unfortunately for the Confederates, the battery's commander was wounded early on. The battery was able to maintain its position, even with the loss of its commander, until the ammunition was spent. With no leadership or ammunition, Ralston's battery fell back. Mouton and his men were pushed back to Labadieville. Once in Labadieville, Mouton was able to reposition his men using a small bridge. He pulled most of his men from the east bank to establish a stronger line on the west bank. It seems he also attempted to create a ruse when he left a considerable smaller force on the east bank in an effort to keep Weitzel busy. The ruse apparently worked. Weitzel chased the smaller force on the east side of Bayou Lafourche for nearly an hour before realizing that the Rebels had given him the slip. One of Weitzel's men described the debacle:

> As we entered [the cane field] *everything was hid from view, and there was little noise beyond the breaking of the stalks as we vainly endeavored to keep in line, forcing our way through the well-nigh impenetrable growth. Nothing but the regimental colors was visible above it. Momentarily we expected the flash of hostile rifles in our faces; yet it was simply impossible to*

keep a regimental line. Without order to that effect the companies gradually fell into a flank movement, and then into one rank, advancing irregularly by the right of companies to the front. Several of the deep draining ditches which cross the fields at right angles were a momentary obstacle. Had the enemy indeed been posted in the field, we must have retired worsted; for we were broken completely into a long single file, and it was impossible to see half-a-dozen rods ahead.

Being alerted by couriers that Mouton had positioned a battery near the bridge where he crossed, Weitzel ordered two flatboats to be pulled downriver to his position. The Confederate battery held its position on the bridge but did not begin firing immediately at the flatboats. The rationale was probably to conserve their ammunition and thinking that they would have plenty of time to take aim at the Yankees while they were ferrying across the bayou, one boatload at a time. However, in an ingenious move, Weitzel did not use the boats to ferry his men across the bayou as expected. The general ordered the boats to be positioned end to end and created a floating bridge across the bayou.

The startled Rebels were taken aback by the move and rushed to reposition and fire at the encroaching Federals. Yet because of their haste, the Confederates commonly overshot the impromptu bridge, missing the Union men completely. Once on the west bank of the bayou, Weitzel's men pushed on, and the battle moved into an open field. The field was bordered by the bayou and its levee on one side and a dense patch of swamp on the other. Mouton used the dense swamp to his advantage and took position just inside the tree line. From this vantage point, the Confederates could easily sight their enemy, but the Yankees were unable to take aim. Undeterred by the Confederates' new position, the Federals pushed forward even though they were being easily picked off. The center of Mouton's line was composed of the Eighteenth Louisiana and the Crescent Regiments, which entrenched themselves in a drainage ditch. Like their fellow soldiers in the swamp, the two regiments held a strong position and were able to easily sight a pick off the encroaching Federals. However, the position was not strong enough. The Union army pushed forward. A Union soldier described the advance:

The enemy's infantry opened upon us with a rattle like the discharge of an endless string of fire-crackers. The invisible messengers came humming and singing in our ear, and striking a man here and there with a quick chuck! That sounded far uglier than the rush of the larger missiles...We passed the band of the Thirteenth Connecticut, and some of the drum-corps, not standing up or, marching to the front blowing and drumming as if their life depended on it, as one sees them represented in picture; but laying flat on the ground behind stumps, and clinging fondly to mother earth.

The Twelfth Connecticut made it within one hundred yards of the ditch before the Confederates retreated from the ditch into the safety of the swamp. In an attempt to slow the Federal advance, the Second Louisiana Cavalry attacked the Union baggage guards, but this attack was short-lived when the cavalry faced off with the Eighth New Hampshire. Seeing that the day was lost, Mouton and his men abandoned the fight and retreated. Weitzel pursued the retreating Rebels for about thirty minutes, until he called off the pursuit and ordered his men back to Donaldsonville. Mouton retreated as far south as Thibodaux.

Though the two armies fought head to head in an open field of battle, neither side sustained heavy losses. The Union lost 74 wounded, 18 killed and 5 captured or missing. The Confederates lost 58 wounded, 5 killed and 186 captured. However, the Confederates lost a lot more in the way of ground. The Confederates retreated back to Thibodaux and opened the top portion of Bayou Lafourche for about thirty-five miles to the Union.

Chapter 16

A Union Soldier's Masonic Burial in Bayou Sara

One event that occurred in Bayou Sara during the Siege of Port Hudson has been nearly lost to history. St. Francisville and Bayou Sara came under siege during June 1863. While shelling the town, a young Union lieutenant was found dead on the USS *Albatross*. Though death during a siege is by no means uncommon, the circumstances surrounding the lieutenant's death were somewhat unusual. Furthermore, his burial itself was anything but common.

The young lieutenant was John E. Hart of Schenectady, New York. He was a career naval officer, a career that spanned more than twenty years. Hart traveled the world with the U.S. Navy. He was even aboard the USS *Constitution* when it circumnavigated the globe in 1846. On October 29, 1862, Hart was given command of the USS *Albatross*. Seven months later, Hart and his crew were engaging and successfully disabling Confederate ships when he received his orders to patrol the Mississippi River above Port Hudson near Bayou Sara.

So when the able-bodied commander was found dead in his stateroom, it came as a surprise to his crew. Reports vary about the cause of Hart's death. They range from simply dying in battle to yellow fever. However, the most accepted cause of the commander's death is suicide. According to the ship's acting surgeon, Hart did suffer from yellow fever, an ailment that commonly caused the commander to struggle with bouts of delirium and depression.

Some years prior to his death, Hart was inducted into the Freemasons. He was a member of St. George's Lodge No. 6 in Schenectady, where his father-in-law was the lodge master. Whether or not he discussed his freemasonry is relatively unknown; what was known to his crew was that their commander wanted a Masonic burial.

Therefore, during the early morning hours after Hart's death, the ship's executive officer, Theodore DuBois, went ashore in search of any local Masons in or around Bayou Sara. Dubois found the White brothers. They were natives of Indiana and members of a northern lodge but told DuBois about the Feliciana Lodge No. 31, only about a mile from the river in the town of St. Francisville. The lodge's master was away serving in the Confederate army, but the Lodge's senior warden and acting master, W.W. Leake, was located nearby. When the White brothers proposed the idea of Leake conducting the Masonic burial for the Yankee commander, Leake said, "As a Mason it is my duty to accord a Masonic burial to a brother Manson without taking into account the nature of our relation in the world outside Masonry. Go tell that Union officer to bring his Captain's body ashore. There are a few Masons left in town; most of us are at the front. I shall assemble all I can." With Leake's approval and the two sides under the flag of truce, the Masonic funeral was set to take place.

On the afternoon of June 13, Leake, the White brothers and three other members of the local lodge gathered at the top of a hill to meet the crew of the *Albatross*. From the gunship, Dr. Burge, Executive Officer DuBois and one other Mason, along with fifty crew members, transported their fallen commander from the gunship to the top of the hill. The members of the two groups introduced themselves and then proceeded to St. Francisville. There are conflicting documents on exactly how the funeral service for Commander Hart was conducted, but these documents do agree that Masonic rites were administered by Leake, and the pastor of Grace Episcopal Church, Reverend Dr. Lewis, read the Episcopal service. A wooden head plate marked the commander's resting place until a grave marker was erected for Hart. The marker read, "This monument is dedicated in loving tribute to the universality of Freemasonry."

After the service, the Union men expressed their appreciation for the hospitality of the local masons and then headed back to the river and boarded the *Albatross*. The *Albatross* left Bayou Sara to meet with the *Hartford* and then sailed farther south to Port Hudson, where it participated in the siege and shelling of the Confederate stronghold. This siege would be the longest during the Civil War and would be the deciding factor of who would ultimately capture the Mississippi River.

As for Leake, he became master of the Feliciana Lodge No. 31. Every year until his death, Leake placed flowers on the Union commander's grave.

Leake died in 1912, and since his death, the town has carried on his tradition. Not only are flowers placed on Hart's grave, but one Saturday every June, the town of St. Francisville commemorates this brief pause in the war in its annual *The Day the War Stopped* program. During the program, a lunch is held at the local Masonic lodge and a reenactment of the procession and burial of John E. Hart takes place.

Chapter 17
Siege of Port Hudson

With the Union now in Baton Rouge and everything south, along with Bayou Sara and its major railroad depot, the Federals set their sights on the most strategic location in the area: Port Hudson. In terms of military strategy, Port Hudson was prime real estate. The Confederate stronghold rested on top of bluffs that overlooked the river. Moreover, Port Hudson had a direct line of sight on a hairpin bend on the river, which enabled the batteries to protect the entire riverfront. The fortification only bolstered about 7,500 men. Meanwhile, the Rebels were up against the combined forces of the XIX Corps and the Army of the Gulf. By combining these two units, the Federals had a fighting force that was upward of 40,000 strong. Though the fighting force at Port Hudson was small, the strategic advantage of its location somewhat made up for it. Not only did the artillery have a fantastic vantage point on the bend in the river, but the high bluffs and outside angle also provided for extreme cannon range up- and downstream. These qualities would be the most valuable assets to the Confederates at Port Hudson during the upcoming siege.

Brigadier General W.N.R. Beall oversaw the building of the land defenses of the area. Though other defenses were being built when Beall was placed in charge of building the defenses, he decided to scrap most of those projects for the idea of building a continuous indented line of parapets and ditches. The line began two and a half miles south of the city and ran north through broken terrain that consisted of a series of fields, ridges and ravines, finally stopping only a mile and a half from a small tributary known as Little Sandy Creek. In total, the Confederate line stretched for more than four miles.

According to most military engineers of the time, such a fortification would require at least fifteen thousand men to hold that position, with upward of another five thousand men in reserves. Unfortunately for the Confederates, they would not even have one-third of those required troops. With an estimated seven thousand men, the Confederates were at a clear disadvantage in terms of manpower. From the time construction began until Banks began shelling the garrison, it took nine months to complete the defenses. However, to complete such a large task in such a short time frame, the construction was built quickly and sometimes rather poorly.

While the land defenses were being constructed, Major General Breckinridge took a Kentucky regiment on an expedition to transport guns back to Port Hudson. Since the ironclad *Essex* was lurking up and down the river near the garrison, it would have been nearly impossible to transport the guns by ship. Therefore, the Confederates only had one option: the guns would have to be transported over land through the broken terrain that surrounded the town. This overland route slowed the arrival of the weapons down to a crawl. However, by the fall and winter of 1862, the heavy guns began to arrive for the river batteries. More began to slowly trickle in afterward. By the time the siege began, Port Hudson was only equipped with nineteen heavy guns: two ten-inch Columbiads, an eight-inch Columbiad, an eight-inch Howitzer, a rifled thirty-two-pounder, five rifled twenty-four-pounders, a thirty-pound Parrott, a twenty-pound Parrott, two forty-two-pound smoothbores, two thirty-two-pound smoothbores, two twenty-four-pound smoothbores and one twelve-pound rifled piece. This stock of artillery was a far cry from the one-hundred-gun armament that was common for fortifications of comparable size to Port Hudson. However, the Rebels made good use of the weapons at their disposal. One of the ten-inch Columbiads was said to have been nicknamed the Demoralizer by the Union troops. The gun was used so effectively and possessed such a long range that the Yankees believed it was mounted on a railroad car and moved to different positions.

The fall of 1862 was a busy period at Port Hudson. Not only did the guns begin to trickle in, but the provisions and supplies began to arrive as well. Port Hudson had always been busy even when it was not a military outpost. Goods from across the state, even across the country, were loaded and unloaded from the dock at Port Hudson. It was in the midst of these business transactions that the garrison was most vulnerable. Due to the hustle and bustle of the busy river town, it was easy for Federal spies to cross the enemy lines and blend in with the multitude of boatmen, speculators and peddlers. However, these missions of espionage were solely assigned to the men. Lieutenant Howard C. Wright, a soldier stationed at Port Hudson, writes about an incident when two women traveling from across the river stopped at Port Hudson. One of the travelers was described as young and quite pretty, while the other was older and apparently in mourning by the way she was dressed. The two did not stay long. Nevertheless, the soldiers were quickly smitten with the younger of the two travelers and set out to impress her with tales of how far the guns could fire, steadfastness of their defenses and any other tale of battle that would impress a young lady. By morning, the two were gone. It was later discovered that the two were Union spies, and any information relayed to them by the men had been turned over to the Federals. Unfortunately, there was little the Confederates could do about such intrusions aside from revealing as little information as possible to the traveling strangers coming and going.

Not only was there a steady stream of people traveling to Port Hudson, but a steady stream of steamboats was constantly loading and unloading cargo as well. It would seem that with such a commercially active river town incorporated into the garrison, Port Hudson should have been well stocked and provisioned, yet this was not the case. The Confederates were plagued with problems when it came to their provisions. The problems became so bad that one officer stated, "If Port Hudson falls, we will have to thank the Commissary Department for it." It seems that the garrison was subject to the whims of bureaucracy. Nothing could be bought without the approval of the Commissary Department. Even the building of warehouses and storehouses was subject to the department that was quickly becoming hated by the troops. Hundreds, possibly thousands, of pounds of food were left to rot even before the siege began. Provisions such as corn and pork rotted in the cargo holds of ships or on loading docks because there was no place to store them. When places were used to store food, they were usually inadequate buildings such as open-air sheds. Such buildings did not protect the provisions from the elements, and often the food would still mold and spoil. Going into the siege, the Confederates were only able to secure three hundred head of beef, four hundred head of sheep and four hundred bushels of corn.

In early May 1863, the Confederacy called for the evacuation of the town of Port Hudson. For the most part, all commerce ceased in the town, turning the area into strictly a military outpost. News quickly spread throughout the garrison that a Federal fleet had been able to make it past the heavy guns at Vicksburg and was headed to Port Hudson. Once it was south of Vicksburg, the fleet was able to quickly sail downriver. By May 8, it was spotted only four and a half miles upriver from the garrison. Later that afternoon, the

Battle of Port Hudson. *Courtesy of Library of Congress, Prints and Photographs Division.*

fleet reached Port Hudson and began ranging its guns. Shortly after, the fleet began its bombardment of the garrison. This bombardment continued every night starting on May 18 and not ending until mid-June. Only on two occasions did the Union pause its nightly bombardment of Port Hudson and fire during the late afternoon. Though the ships often shelled the garrison during the day, these two occasions were the only times they did not shell at night. The sporadic schedule of the bombardment and the preference toward nighttime shelling was not only to damage the fortification but also to keep the Confederates from getting any sleep.

Not allowing the enemy to sleep was the only real advantage that could be attributed to the fleet's bombardment. The total number of casualties that was a direct result of the fleet's shells during the forty-three days of bombardment was four dead and three wounded. Two of those wounded eventually lost a leg each. Though the casualty rate was low, the shelling of Port Hudson was by no means easy on the Confederates. The shells may not have killed many of the Rebels, but they effectively destroyed roads and buildings. On occasion, the shelling actually worked in the favor of the Confederates. On one such occasion during the latter part of the siege, a shell missed its mark, landed in the river and exploded underwater. To the Rebels' delight, the underwater explosion killed nearly eighty fish, causing them to float to the river's surface. Many of the besieged men paddled out into the river to collect as many of the fish as they could. This was an added bonus for the Confederates because they would often pay anywhere from five to fifty dollars for fish, depending on the size. These rare occasions aside, the Federal navy did kept General Franklin Gardener and his men busy, but it was the land forces that stood to cause the most damage.

Chapter 18
The Battle of Plains Store

On the morning of May 21, 1863, Major General Christopher C. Augur, leading the First Division of the XIX Corps, was traveling from Baton Rouge toward the intersection of Plains Store and Bayou Sara Roads. The Union division was on its way to secure a river landing for Major General Nathaniel Banks. Banks was on his way with the other three divisions of the XIX Corps—all four divisions totaling thirty-six thousand men—to prepare a siege on Port Hudson.

Also in the area was Colonel Benjamin H. Grierson's cavalry, which was composed of Sixth and Seventh Illinois Cavalries. Grierson, a thirty-six-year-old former music teacher, had gained quite the reputation as a cavalry commander. Major General William T. Sherman described him as "the best cavalry commander I have yet had." He gained notoriety in 1863 when he executed what would become known as Grierson's raid. The raid lasted from April 17 to May 2, 1863, and encompassed more than six hundred miles. The Union needed a diversion from Major General Ulysses S. Grant's main attack plan on Vicksburg, Mississippi, and Grant thought that Grierson's cavalry was exactly what he needed.

Grierson executed the diversion flawlessly and was able to do what no other Union cavalry could. Although he was rumored to hate horses, he commanded 1,700 horse troopers from southern Tennessee, across the entire state of Mississippi and on to Union-held Baton Rouge. On their southern trek, Grierson's cavalry destroyed railroads and bridges, burned Confederate storehouses and other buildings and freed a number of slaves.

Christopher Auger. *Courtesy of National Archives and Records Administration.*

Benjamin Grierson. *Courtesy of Library of Congress, Prints and Photographs Division.*

Nevertheless, Augur's movements gained the attention of General Franklin Gardener, who was overseeing the reinforcing of Port Hudson. Believing the movement of Union troops could be a sign of something greater, Gardener dispatched a detachment of the Fourteenth Arkansas under the command of Colonel Powers. This included a small cavalry force and Abbay's Mississippi Battery. Powers and Grierson encountered each other near a crossroads near a two-story building that housed Young's store and the Plains Masonic

Franklin Gardener.

Lodge. Immediately, a skirmish ensued that lasted the greater part of the morning. The Federals tried to move up the plain but were kept at bay by the guns of the Mississippi battery. Colonel Nathan Augustus Monroe Dudley responded to the Confederate artillery by firing his own artillery. The two artillery units traded fire for nearly two hours.

Around lunchtime, Powers sent for reinforcements, and Colonel W.R. Miles was underway with nearly four hundred men of the Louisiana Legion. However, by the time Miles reached his cohorts, the outmanned and outgunned 14th Arkansas had already retreated. Even though Powers and the 14th Arkansas retreated back to Port Hudson, Miles saw an opportunity to take the Union troops by surprise. By arriving so late in the day, Miles caught the Union troops in the midst of making camp for the night. Encountering the 48th Massachusetts positioned on Port Hudson road, Miles fired a combination of artillery and musketry. The barrage took the Union troops by surprise and scattered them. Immediately, Dudley ordered the 49th Massachusetts and the 116th New York to aid the startled regiment. However, another round of gunfire once again caught the Union off guard and sent the entire camp into chaos.

This initial ambush allowed the Confederates to drive the Union back into a thickly wooded area. Under the cover of the dense forest, the Union was able to regroup. The Confederates thought they may have seized the day when Lieutenant Colonel F.B. Brand was able to flank the 116th New York, but the Yankee soldiers were able to about-face and return fire. The 116th then began to drive back Brand and his men. The three Confederate companies were pushed back into an open field. Though they attempted to hold their ground, Brand and Miles were pushed into another section of heavily wooded terrain. With one final push, Dudley's men were able to dislodge the Confederates, forcing Miles to retreat back to Port Hudson, which ended the battle.

Though he started out with the element of surprise, Miles could not stand against the overwhelming Union force. After arriving back in Port

Hudson, Miles submitted his report: eighty-nine killed, wounded and missing. However, even though the Union was victorious in this battle, it did not walk away from it unscathed. It was reported that the Union side sustained fifteen killed, seventy-one wounded and fourteen captured. Prior to issuing the report, a large number of Union soldiers was reported as missing. Shortly after, many of them were discovered sneaking back to Baton Rouge and possibly attempting to desert. Some historians speculate that this large number of Union deserters is due to the fact that many of those soldiers were young and the Battle of Plains Store, an overall footnote in the Civil War, was the first time many of them had seen battle. In John D. Winters's account, *The Civil War in Louisiana*, he states, "For most of the Federal troops, this was their first time under fire, and they ducked and dodged at the sound of the shells overhead. When wounded men and bleeding horses were seen coming from the front line, many of the troops felt their first great fear of battle."

Essentially, it is still not exactly known what either side expected to accomplish in the Battle of Plains Store. The entire affair played out with no real objective in sight. Initially, the small Confederate detachment was ineffective against Major General Augur's First Division of the XIX Corps. By the time Miles arrived with reinforcements, the fight of the day had ended. Again, with no real objective in mind except to wreak havoc and chaos on the Union troops, Miles attacked. In hindsight, it seems that Miles should have known that once the Union forces were able to regroup, he would have been no match for such a force. The Union's goal could have simply been to maintain the mission: to secure a river landing for Major General Nathaniel Banks and the other three divisions of the XIX Corps. This is exactly what they did. On May 22, around 2:00

Nathaniel Banks. *Courtesy of Library of Congress, Prints and Photographs Division.*

a.m., Banks landed his men near Bayou Sara. His landing was uneventful, and he unloaded his troops unopposed.

Even though this battle seemed like a random event with no real goal in mind, most historians agree that the Union victory resulted in a positive reward for the Federals. This victory allowed the Union to effectively close that last Confederate escape route out of Port Hudson. However, as time will tell, this would be no easy battle. Port Hudson did not fall as quickly as Baton Rouge or New Orleans had. Gardener spent weeks prior to the Battle of Plains Store fortifying his garrison and gathering supplies. Just across the river, even in the presence of Federal gunboats, it has been estimated that Gardener was able to acquire three hundred head of cattle, four hundred sheep and four hundred bushels of corn. These estimates do not account for the supplies that he was able to acquire from the east.

With a fortified garrison, no escape route leading out of the Confederate garrison and the full force of Nathaniel Banks's men only a few miles north of Port Hudson, near Thompson's Creek, the stage was set for the Siege of Port Hudson to begin.

On the morning of May 27, the Federals began to bombard the Confederate left and center. Thirty minutes later, Weitzel led 6,000 men

U.S. artillery at the Siege of Port Hudson. *Courtesy of National Archives and Records Administration.*

in an attack on 1,200 Confederate troops near Little Sandy Creek. The overwhelmed and clearly outnumbered Confederates were pushed back into their works. Nevertheless, the determined Rebels were in a position to decimate their Northern adversaries. Confederate colonel W.R. Miles noticed how outnumbered his men were. To try to bolster their spirits, he yelled out to his men, "Shoot low, boys; it takes two men to take away a man who is wounded, and they never come back." As the Union army tried to regroup on a nearby ridge, the entrenched Confederates opened fire. The Yankee troops tried to charge but were quickly mowed down by the Confederate barrage. Even the Union artillery was no match for the Confederates. As the artillery began to unlimber on the ridge, the entrenched men fired, tearing the cannon crew to shreds.

As cannons fired back and forth during what was to become a hellacious ordeal for both sides, one position in particular took a significant beating from the Union assault. On the northeast corner of the Union lines, the Confederates built a lunette on top of a ridge. The men at this position had to face several attacks, during many of which they were outnumbered, during the May 27 assault on Port Hudson. The position was such a challenge to defend that the men stationed there quickly nicknamed the lunette Fort Desperate.

The men charged with defending this position were of the Fifteenth Arkansas Infantry Regiment. Colonel Benjamin Whitfield Johnson commanded the regiment. The odds were stacked against the regiment from the very start of their service at Port Hudson. Initially, the Fifteenth Arkansas was positioned on the center of the Confederate line. However, in a last-minute decision, Colonel I.G.W. Steedman ordered Johnson to relocate his men from the center to a ridge located on the Confederate left. When Johnson and his men arrived at the ridge, they found that no defensive structures had been built. Steedman's snap decision only gave the Fifteenth Arkansas six days to construct some sort of defensive fortification.

Well aware that a Union strike was quickly approaching, Johnson immediately ordered his men to begin work on a fortification. The men built a large, solid parapet that protected their camp on three sides. After the parapet was completed, they were ordered to dig a trench on the outside of the wall that ran along the parapet's length. The parapet and the trench, though simple in design, were used in tandem to create a formidable lunette that stretched for a quarter mile. The terrain leading down the ridge was a steep slope, which would naturally slow the approach of the Union troops. However, to slow their approach even further, Johnson ordered large amounts of timber to be cut and brush to be gathered. The timber and brush was littered down the sides of the ridge's slopes to serve as obstacles for any advancing Federal armies.

Aiding the defense of Fort Desperate were two small detachments from Captain Andrew Herod's First Mississippi Battery B, which were each equipped with a twelve-pound howitzer. Since these two guns were the only artillery at Johnson's disposal, the colonel set out to use them in the most efficient way possible. He placed the guns on each end of the crescent-shaped fortification and had them loaded with canister. Though the fortification was hastily built and would require constant repairs throughout the siege, it was completed before Banks could initiate his attacks. The Fifteenth Arkansas was ready to defend its position when Port Hudson was fired upon on May 27.

Though the men of the 15th Arkansas were outnumbered, they were able to ward off the various Union assaults that occurred throughout the day. One such assault occurred when General Grover attempted to break the Confederate line in the northeast position. The general ordered the 159th New York to attack the Confederates' left flank. Even though they sustained heavy losses and casualties, the men of the 159th were able to make it within thirty yards of the lunette's trenches. Nevertheless, the Federals were not able to advance any farther. Johnson's 15th was able to force the Federals to take cover in an available ravine or gully. Some were even forced to lay behind the very timbers used to slow the Yankee advance. With the 159th New York pinned down, Grover attempted a two-pronged assault that would break the line and aid the New Yorkers. He ordered the 12th Maine, 13th Connecticut and 25th Connecticut to charge up the face and the left side of the ridge at the same time.

The idea behind this was that the outnumbered Rebels would be overwhelmed and could not keep the assaulting force at bay. Initially, the plan seemed like it was going to work. While the other regiments were being held back, the men of the 12th Maine were able to fight all the way to the walls of Fort Desperate and plant their flag. However, the Rebel troops immediately stormed out of the lunette in an effort to drive the Yankees back, and they were successful. After a round of hand-to-hand and bayonet fighting, the 15th Arkansas was able to drive back the 12th Maine. Just like the 159th New York, the men of the Maine were forced to seek cover in any available ravine or gully. The Union's new position did not cause much harm to the Confederate lunette, with the exception of the occasional rifle fire that raked across Fort Desperate.

The men inside Fort Desperate were able to ward off the attacks for most of the morning. The steep slopes definitely slowed down the assaulting Federals. The steady fire of the Fifteenth Arkansas, compounded by the barrage of canister, kept the Union troops pinned down. Unfortunately for Johnson, Fort Desperate did not come out of the battle completely unscathed. One of the howitzers was hit, killing its commander, Lieutenant Jesse Edrington.

Even though Fort Desperate sustained quite a bit of damage, lost forty men and temporarily lost a cannon (the howitzer was repaired and placed back in service a couple days later), the Fifteenth Arkansas caused a considerable amount more damage to the Federals. Colonel Johnson reported that his regiment killed ninety men while wounding more than three hundred. It seems that against all odds, Fort Desperate withstood its first challenge. However, the men would have to go up against the Union force again on June 13.

By 10:00 a.m. on May 27, the soldiers of the Union army had not made any progress. In an attempt to organize their charge, they began a series of two-regiment attacks. Two regiments made up of Louisiana free blacks and former slaves made the first attempt. After this initial attempt failed, three more two-regiment attacks ensued. All of them failed. None of the attacks made the slightest dent in Port Hudson's defenses. Realizing failure, the attacks were called off around noon. The Union lost seven hundred men to either death or wounds during the four two-regiment attacks. Though the attacks were called off, the Confederates could not rest easy. Banks immediately ordered a renewed bombardment of the garrison. This bombardment consisted of thirty cannons that focused on the left and center that was being held by Brigadier General Beall. Beall tried to reply to the Union bombardment with cannon fire of his own, but realizing that his return fire was having little effect on the Union, he called off the return fire.

The bombardment of Port Hudson continued, but little advancement was made by the Union. Federal sharpshooters were positioned throughout the area, which forced the Confederates to keep their heads down. After sustaining so many casualties, it seems that Nathaniel Banks felt the need to justify his actions. He writes, "If I defend New Orleans and its adjacent; the enemy will go against Grant. If I go with force to aid him they will go against my rear."

On June 5, 1863, General Paine left Port Hudson with about 4,000 men, along with a large artillery force, in an effort to aid Grierson. Two days prior to Paine's departure, Grierson had been sent to Clinton, Louisiana, with roughly 1,200 soldiers to break John Logan's grip on the area. The Federal cavalry crossed the Comite River and then made it to a location known as Pretty Creek with few problems. However, Grierson's lack of problems quickly changed when he stumbled upon Colonel Powers, who was in command of Cage's Louisiana battalion and Garland's troops. With this combined force, Powers was able to strike at Grierson's left flank and rear, taking the Federal cavalry by total surprise. This initial attack, along with a strong charge from Major John Stockdale, pushed Grierson's men across the Amite River. It was on the banks of the Amite that Grierson was able to maintain a strong position to wait for Paine's reinforcements.

By June 7, the Union cavalry had moved into the town of Clinton. Paine met Grierson in Clinton only to discover that the town was virtually deserted, with the exception of the awaiting cavalry. It seems Logan was aware of the pending Union attack and had retreated ten miles north of the area. Logan's escape would allow him to lead the Third Division of James B. McPherson's XVII Corps into Vicksburg. It was this division that was first to enter the city of Vicksburg after its capture. Logan would then go on to serve as its military governor.

Even though the Confederates vacated the town, it did not stop the Union from setting fire to anything useful the town had to offer. Grierson and his men set fire to the train depot, a locomotive and a machine shop. Other buildings that they set fire to were a wooden mill and a warehouse. The troops did not just set fire to buildings. It was reported that the Union also set fire to a supply of corn, ammunition and several hundred barrels of rum.

With much of the town reduced to ashes and Logan out of the area, the Union troops had no choice but to return to Port Hudson to help with the ongoing siege. However, this would not be the only skirmish that would take place near Clinton. The parish seat would see several other skirmishes right up until the end of the war. The last skirmish occurred only one month prior to the close of the Civil War.

In mid-June, Banks seemed to have caught a break. A Confederate deserter informed him that the men in the garrison were sick, hungry and demoralized. Though the Confederates were holding their position, they were maintaining it with only four thousand men. Moreover, Banks learned that Gardener had been forced to divide his artillery. Six heavy guns were moved to help ward off the land attacks, leaving only thirteen aimed at the river to protect against Farragut's powerful fleet. With this information in hand, Banks began planning for a second attack. The second attack would also be helped by the newest addition to Banks's arsenal, a twenty-four-barrel Gatling gun. However, for this new plan to work, his assault troops needed an easily maneuverable path through the heavily wooded and broken terrain. To create the path, Banks relied on volunteer regiments known as "forlorn hope" units. These men were armed with only shovels, saws, planks and poles. They carried with them three-foot bags that were stuffed with cotton. Their mission was to clear a path and bridge any ditch or ravine that stood in the way.

On June 13, Banks began his renewed attacks. He led this initiative with a period of heavy bombardment. During this bombardment, it has been estimated that the Union artillery was able to fire a shell every second. Confident that this instilled fear into the besieged men, Banks stopped the bombardment and issued an ultimatum: surrender or sustain another bombardment. It did not take long for Gardener to refuse the ultimatum. Banks ordered the bombardment to continue, and it did throughout the night until the next morning.

Around 4:00 a.m. on the morning of June 14, Paine's division attacked a portion of Beall's line near a strong fortification known as Priest Cap. Immediately, the Confederates opened fire. This fire was later described as being so intense that the hill was "shaved bald, every blade of grass cut down to the roots." Several Union soldiers did make it to the parapets but were quickly killed or captured. Paine was wounded in the attack as well.

Even though the attack was easily repelled by the Confederates, Weitzel made another attempt around 8:00 a.m. The second attempt was quickly foiled when the fire from the Confederates forced Weitzel's men down into a ravine. The stranded Federals were swept by gunfire from Fort Desperate and Priest Cap. Two additional regiments were sent to aid the men, but those regiments were quickly pinned down by the Confederates as well. Auger carried out his assault on the Rebel center but had no more success than Weitzel. Auger's attack was repelled just as the attacks before him.

As the day ended, so did the assaults on the garrison. Though several attempts were made, the Union could not take Port Hudson. Banks reported that he lost 1,800 men—a staggering loss, especially when compared to Gardener's 47 casualties. As the day came to a close, Banks refused a truce to allow the Confederates to bury their dead and immediately began another bombardment. However, the smell of death in a Louisiana summer became so powerful that it forced a cease-fire between the two armies. Three days after the attacks, the Confederates were allowed to bury their fallen. Never missing an opportunity to cause the Yankees as much discomfort as possible, most of the dead were buried near Union lines.

After the cease-fire, things began to settle down, and an informal, unofficial truce was maintained. The Union bombardment slowed to a near stop. This truce was to the benefit of both sides. Both Union and Confederate were running dangerously low on supplies. This was especially the case for ammunition, especially in the Confederate camp. Several guns were dismounted during the June 14 attacks. The shells were fashioned into hand grenades in an attempt to make up for the lack of firepower. The cease-fire also allowed the two sides to reinforce their fortifications.

Chapter 19

The Battle at Jackson Crossroads

In the midst of the Siege of Port Hudson, nearly two hundred Union wagons headed to Jackson, Louisiana, on the morning of June 20. The main purpose of this expedition was to forage the area for supplies, mainly cotton, to be used on the Federal siege lines. The wagon train was being escorted through the countryside by Company E, Fifty-second Regiment, Massachusetts Volunteers, which was commanded by Colonel Halbert Greenleaf. Greenleaf had been a lock manufacturer and a captain for the Massachusetts Militia prior to the war. He enlisted in the Union army and quickly worked his way up the ranks. Not even a week prior to this expedition, Greenleaf had lost three men killed and seven wounded.

When the two-mile-long wagon train reached the Jackson-Clinton road, it was taken by surprise by Colonel Thomas R. Stockdale who commanded the Mississippi Cavalry Battalion. The ambush terrified the mules pulling the wagons, causing a massive stampede. Many of the wagons were lost or destroyed in the chaos. Nevertheless, the stampede was the perfect distraction for Stockdale, who was able to win the skirmish quickly and easily. The spoils were great. When the dust settled, the Mississippi Cavalry Battalion took fifty wagons, two hundred mules and fifty prisoners. Greenleaf and his men returned to the siege lines of Port Hudson and remained there until its capture.

It was during fortification of its defenses that the Union built one of the more interesting breastworks at Port Hudson. The structure became known as the Great Cotton Bale Battery. With limited supplies, including building materials, the Union had to make use of any and all materials that were on hand. The men built saps and towers from empty barrels. Miles of walkways made from discarded materials navigated the Federal lines. However, Major Joseph Bailey, an engineer by trade, noticed an abundance of cotton bales. Bailey designed a battery that was constructed primarily of the cotton bales. The structure took his men two weeks to build.

It was decided that the structure would be best located 250 yards from a ravine that ran directly in front of Battery No. 11, which was commonly referred to as the Citadel by the Union troops. The Great Cotton Bale Battery, or "Bailey's Battery," consisted of a main structure with two smaller emplacements on either side. In total, the battery held seventeen guns. The plan was to use the battery to pound the Confederates into submission. Though the battery stood firm and blasted away, the structure also had its drawbacks. One was its sheer size. By building a large, easily sighted structure, the Union gave its opponents an easy target at which to fire. The smoke from the guns was an obstacle to the crews in the battery but also for the spotters who directed the fire for the mortar boats anchored at the river below. Drawbacks aside, Bailey's Battery became a crucial fixture in the Siege of Port Hudson. On the afternoon of June 26, the guns of the battery began their bombardment of the Citadel. Due to the position of the battery, the Confederates could not utilize the full force of their heavy guns. Nevertheless, Lieutenant Colonel Paul F. DeGourney was able to put nineteen holes in the Union flag and another in the arm of Major Roy, who was commanding the battery.

The battery was not the only construction going on at the Union line. A sap was being dug from the battery to the foot of Battery No. 11. After the initial bombardment ended, men from the 165th New York and the 6th Michigan charged up the hill that led to the Citadel. These men were quickly pinned down by Confederate fire. Many of these men remained pinned down for the rest of the night and well into the following day. Even by the following day, the men had to make a mad dash for the sap. General Dwight, who was not satisfied with this first attempt and appeared drunk, ordered the two regiments to storm the fortification again. Instead of just being pinned this time, many of the men became easy targets. Union soldiers were plucked from the hillside left and right. A few men did make it to the Confederate works, only to be killed immediately. The troops named this failed attack the Whiskey Charge due to Dwight's drunken state when the order was given.

The Union navy was not much help to the men in Bailey's Battery. Because of the smoke produced by the guns, the mortar boats could not effectively hit their mark. Throughout the day, the gunboats often overshot their targets and wounded their own men. It was reported that Farragut's fleet killed more Union soldiers that day than all the Confederate troops killed throughout the entire siege. Though it was an engineering marvel, the Great Cotton Bale Battery could not bring down the Confederates. However, the Confederates could not rest easy. The siege was far from over, and they had a new problem to deal with. On top of the Union bombardments and charges on the garrison, by June 29, the last quarter ration of beef had been issued. The Confederate provisions were severely depleted.

Chapter 20

The Second Battle of Donaldsonville

The Federals had occupied Donaldsonville since their initial bombardment of the town more than a year earlier. During that time, they had enough time to construct Fort Butler. It was from this fort that the Union based its operations into the Lafourche region. The fort itself was built on the banks of Bayou Lafourche where it forked away from the Mississippi River. During this time, Bayou Lafourche was a large, navigable waterway that allowed steamers to travel from the Mississippi River to interior cities such as Thibodaux and emptied into the Gulf of Mexico. Later, in 1905, the bayou was dammed, which reduced the navigable waterway to a large ditch or small canal. Fort Butler was garrisoned by two companies of the Twenty-eighth Maine Volunteer Infantry, which was under the command of Major Joseph D. Bullen.

The fort was an impressive sight that loomed across the bayou from Donaldsonville, and it was well protected. Its engineer, First Lieutenant Ladilas "Louis" Wrotnowski, designed the fortification in the shape of a star. The fort was constructed mostly of brickwork and was protected from the east by the Mississippi River and from the south by Bayou Lafourche. Wrotnowski ordered a moat, sixteen feet wide and twelve feet deep, to encircle the entire fort. The eastern and southern sides of the fort were also equipped with two stockades that stretched from the fort to the banks of the river and bayou. Furthermore, Fort Butler was armed with six twenty-four-pound siege cannons.

On the morning of June 28, 1863, two brigades—Tom Green's Texas Brigade and Colonel James Patrick Major's Texas Brigade—attacked the

Thomas Green.

fort. The two brigades were ordered by Brigadier General Mouton to seize the fort and take back control of Donaldsonville. The plan of attack was outlined in his order:

> *The Fourth, Fifth, and Seventh Regiments Texas Mounted Volunteers, the Second Regiment Louisiana Cavalry, Waller's Battalion, the Valverde Battery and Nichol's Battery will constitute the First Brigade...under the command of General Thomas Green Baylor's Regiment, Stone's Regiment, Gurley's Regiment (30th Texas Partisan Rangers), Philip's Regiment, Speight's Battery, and Semmes Battery will constitute the Second Brigade... General J.P. Majors is assigned...command of the same.*

The plan was to have the Second Cavalry Brigade lead the head column and take the fort head-on. This frontal assault was to distract the Yankees long enough to allow the Fifth Texas to advance from its position toward Fort Butler. The Fifth Texas Mounted Volunteers were to circle around the fort and position themselves on the bank of the Mississippi River about a mile north of the fort. They were to attack on the stockade side nearest the river. The Fifth Texas's goal was to create an entrance near the stockade during the distraction so the Rebels could take the fort from the inside. The Fourth Texas Mounted Volunteers were to execute a similar maneuver but on the bayou side of the fort. Again, while the Union was distracted with the Second Cavalry, the Fourth Texas was to create an entrance near the stockades on the bayou side. The Third Arizona Cavalry, First Texas Partisan Rangers and Seventh Texas Cavalry were to focus their attention on the twenty-four-pound cannons. These men were ordered to position themselves near the sixteen-foot-wide moat and pick off as many members of the Federal cannon crew as possible.

The goal was to complete all this before daybreak so they would not have to deal with the fire of the Union gunboats just offshore. If the Confederates could take the fort before dawn, the gunboats would not fire on it because of the Union men held prisoner inside. Taking the fort would mean regaining control of the town, and then they could maintain control over Bayou Lafourche. Maintaining control over the bayou would take them one step closer to maintaining control of the Mississippi River.

About 1:30 a.m., the Confederates initiated their attack the fort. They moved in a swift, coordinated attack. The head column was drawing the attention of the Union troops, just as Green had anticipated. What Green did not anticipate was the immediate assistance of the Union navy in the form of the USS *Princess Royale*, which weighed anchor and began shelling the assaulting Confederate men. The *Princess Royale* began its naval war career as a Confederate blockade runner but was seized by the Federals in May 1863. The steamship was small, but it boasted a wide array of guns. The USS *Princess Royale* sailed with two thirty-pounder Parrott rifles, one nine-inch Dahlgren smoothbore and four twenty-four-pounder howitzers, which were a welcome sight for the Twenty-eighth Maine. Even though the USS *Princess Royale* rained down shells, the Confederates continued to advance.

The Fifth Texas made it to the riverside stockade and pushed the defenders back. Men were barreling over the outer works and headed straight for the walls. While some men provided cover fire, others began chopping away in an attempt to create a much-needed hole. Many of the men moved to the rear of the fort, where they, too, attempted to force their way in. Minutes later, the USS *Princess Royale* moved in closer and loaded grapeshot. Though its crew could not see, they fired blindly toward the sounds of the Confederates. The Fourth Texas somehow got lost in the darkness and did not make it to the fort until dawn.

Unable to wait, Green ordered the entire line to advance forward. The Confederates moved in the darkness, taking as much ground as they could, with many more crossing the outer work at 2:00 a.m. By this time, Green was confident that he would have Fort Butler in his possession by daybreak.

The Rebels of the Fifth Texas and Third Arizona made it to the outer wall of the fort and began to climb. However, when they made it over, the Confederates found themselves on the banks of an impassable ditch, though many of the men attempted to cross it. They were trapped. The river was at their backs, and this newfound ditch was at their front. The Confederates did everything they could to secure their survival, even throwing loose bricks at their enemy. Many of the men who attempted to forge the ditch were simply picked off by the Twenty-eighth Maine. Between the hail of gunfire coming from the Twenty-eighth Maine and the constant shelling from the *Princess Royale* compounded by the size of the ditch, the Confederates could do nothing but move forward.

The Third Cavalry, Arizona Brigade, made it to the rear rampart of the fort and began to climb. However, when Colonel Joseph Philips was killed in the attempt and Major Alonzo Ridley was captured, most of the men retreated. After the battle, Ridley stated that at least ninety men captured by the Union that night were hiding at the bottom of that twelve-foot moat. By 3:00 a.m., the Confederates on the left and right of the fort had surrendered. The head column had retreated while, amazingly enough, many of the troops who made it past the outer works were able to escape. It seems that the Twenty-eighth Maine survived the attack. However, they were not sure if the Confederates were reorganizing for a second attack. Those worries quickly dissipated when the USS *Kineo* and USS *Winona* dropped anchor. The Confederates would not charge the fort in their presence.

By dawn, it was clear that the Confederates would not be able to take control of Fort Butler. However, what happened next is somewhat lost to history. According to the Union, a band of Rebels approached the fort under the white flag of surrender. As the Union allowed the men to approach, the Rebels fired at them. However, General Green's report described the scene quite differently:

> At daylight I sent the flag of truce, asking permission to pick up our wounded and bury our dead, which I was refused, as I expected. My object in sending a flag so early was to get away a great number of our men who had found little shelter near the enemy's works and who would undoubtedly be taken prisoners. As it turned out, I must have saved a hundred men by instructing my flag of truce officer as he approached the fort to order our troops still there, away.

Bullen immediately requested more men in case the Confederates returned. His request was approved, and he received the remaining two companies of the Twenty-eighth Maine, the First Louisiana and two sections of Closson's Battery.

As a result of the attack, the Federals lost 8 killed and 13 wounded. The Confederates lost 114 wounded, 107 missing and 31 dead. However, this count may not be entirely accurate. Bullen reported that he buried at least 50 Confederates. Many of these men were buried where they had fallen in a mass grave because Green's request was denied. Out of the many who were buried in the grave, barely 30 have been identified. The grave is still visible today and is marked by a gravestone. Etched in the monument is a poem as a memorial to the men who had fallen. It reads:

> *Tenderly bury the fair young dead*
> *Pausing to drop on his grave a tear;*
> *Carve on the wooden slab at his head*
> *Somebody's darling is buried here.*
> —*Marie LeCaste*

The monument was erected by the United Daughters of the Confederacy Fort Butler Monument and dedicated on June 27, 1999.

Chapter 21

The Skirmish at Springfield Landing

B arely a month after the burning of Clinton, Powers was back in town plotting his next move. Wanting to weaken the Union stranglehold on Port Hudson, Powers decided to raid Banks's main supply depot at Springfield Landing. Not only would a successful raid loosen the Federal grip on the garrison, but the mission could also make up for Powers's earlier debacle.

In an earlier effort to ease the Siege of Port Hudson and gather intelligence, Powers and a small group of Confederate scouts had kidnapped General Neal Dow. Prior to the Civil War, Dow was most famous for his actions during the Portland Rum Riot. When he was mayor of Portland, Maine, many of the locals were opposed to and protested his ban on alcohol. Dow ordered the local militia to open fire into the crowd of protesters. The result of the order was one protester killed and seven others wounded. General Dow imposed a similar ban on alcohol on his troops. During the Siege of Port Hudson, Dow was wounded in the right arm and the left thigh and was recovering at a nearby residence. Though Powers was successful in kidnapping the recovering general, it did not have the demoralizing effect on the Union he had hoped for. In reality, taking the general as prisoner had no effect on the Union progress at Port Hudson at all. Dow did not possess any valuable knowledge that the Confederates could have used against Banks, nor did his men like him enough to affect overall morale. It seems that his staunch opposition to the consumption of alcohol caused him to be particularly disliked among the ranks. Powers hoped to rectify his error in judgment by raiding Springfield Landing.

On the night of July 2, Powers left Clinton and traveled south to Springfield Landing. The ultimate goal of the mission was to set fire to the all-important depot, just as the Union had set fire to Clinton. Late that night, Powers's cavalry and a group of mounted partisans were able to take the camp by surprise. The Confederates immediately stormed the camp, setting fire to anything that would burn. The chaos that ensued definitely worked in the favor of the Confederates because the 16th New Hampshire could do nothing but scatter. Federal gunboats began to fire into the camp, but that did not pose much of a deterrent. It was not until the 162nd New York arrived

Neal Dow.

on the scene that Union troops were able to pose a threat to the raiding Confederates. The infantrymen were able to somewhat calm the scene, but not without sustaining some losses to their regiment. The 162nd was able to outnumber and force Powers to fall back to Clinton. However, in the process of pushing back the Confederates, the 162nd New York lost ten men. Overall, the raid on Springfield Landing was a success for Powers. Even though he lost several men and was forced to retreat back to Clinton, the Confederates still caused an estimated total of $1 million in damages.

An interesting footnote to this skirmish is the number of African Americans who were present and killed at Springfield Landing. According to John Winters's *The Civil War in Louisiana*, there were several hundred African Americans present at the supply depot when the skirmish took place. However, it was never clearly stated why they were there, though it seems that they were not there in a militaristic capacity. Nevertheless, a total of twenty-one African Americans were killed during the skirmish. During the initial charge of Powers's men and throughout the burning of Springfield Landing, there was a mad rush made by Union soldiers and the African Americans to the nearby steamboats for safety. As it turns out, this was not the safest area to relocate to. Winters writes that all of the twenty-one African Americans who were killed drowned while attempting to board those steamboats.

With the supplies quickly dwindling at Port Hudson, Gardener had to find some way of sustaining his men. When the last ration of beef was given out, the men resorted to eating horses and rats. He also ordered an injured mule to be slaughtered and prepared. The mule meat quickly became a favorite among the ranks. One soldier described it as "darker in color than beef, of a finer grain, quite tender and juicy, and has a flavor something between beef and venison." Many of the men were discriminatory, or at least tried to be, when it came to eating rats; however, very few turned down their ration of mule meat.

Another Port Hudson delicacy was a weak beer made from the few stores of sugar and molasses that were left. The beverage was so well liked that it became a mainstay on the Confederate lines and was provided to the men by the barrel. The beer's popularity had little to do with its taste. It was actually described as a "weak description." Weak or not, the libation was much easier to swallow than the poor-quality water that was issued. The beer also gave the men some sense of luxury, as miniscule as it was, when every other basic need had been taken from them. It is these improvised provisions that kept many of the Confederates alive after July 4. However, the mule and makeshift beer were only enough to be able to last until mid-July. Most of the men at Port Hudson seemed to prefer dining on mule and weak beer than surrendering their post. Unknown to them at the time, the Confederates would not have a chance to make good on those sentiments.

As the first mule was being carved up on July 4 at Port Hudson, Vicksburg surrendered to Grant. General Gardener and his besieged men would learn of this surrender a few days later.

Chapter 22

The Confederate Surrender of Port Hudson

By the afternoon of July 7, the Confederates knew something was up. They were just uncertain as to what all this new Union activity could mean. Prior to hearing what seemed to be jovial sounds coming from the Federal camp, rumors were circulating throughout Port Hudson that the Yankees were planning another attack. According to this rumor, the Union was going to attack the garrison with at least one thousand men. For the rest of the day, the Rebels could hear the salutes of the mortar boats and the cheers of the crews. These celebratory sounds only solidified the Confederate belief that an attack was on its way. However, in reality, there would be no other attacks on Port Hudson.

The salutes from the gunboats and the cheers of their crews were a direct result of a Federal gunboat bringing news about the Confederate surrender at Vicksburg. The gunboat stopped off and told the upper fleet, which immediately began to salute and cheer. When Colonel Kirby Smith brought the news to Nathaniel Banks, the entire Union line broke into a celebration. Later that day, the lower fleet was told of the fall of Vicksburg; once again, cheers and salutes erupted from the fleet. Union soldiers began calling out to the Rebels, telling them that their brethren in Vicksburg had surrendered.

Upon hearing the news from the enemy, the Confederates were in disbelief. Most of the ranks thought it was a ploy concocted by the Yankees to attempt to crush the spirits of the Confederates while simultaneously raising the spirits of their own. Many were in disbelief because the idea of Vicksburg falling before Port Hudson was unfathomable. No one, including the men in the garrison, ever thought that Port Hudson could outlast Vicksburg. The tiny garrison paled in comparison to Vicksburg. It was poorly manned, armed and provisioned. Port Hudson was only an outpost to Vicksburg. However, this tiny, poorly supplied outpost was the last Confederate stronghold on the lower Mississippi River.

As the fighting seemed to come to a halt, the ranks of either side began to fraternize with one another. This fraternization allowed for the details of Vicksburg's surrender to spread throughout the camp, making the idea of the Confederate stronghold's demise much more plausible among the troops. However, the Confederates, and General Gardener in particular, were not prepared to make any decisions based on the gossip of the idle troops. Therefore, Gardener sent a party out after midnight to request and receive a copy of the official communiqués of General Grant verifying Pemberton's surrender. The Federals complied with Gardener's request. Gardener received the communiqués and began making plans. Even though the communiqués were uncredited, Gardener took heed, and notes were sent back and forth throughout the early morning hours to prepare for the Confederate surrender at Port Hudson.

As Gardener was corresponding with Banks, he was also holding a war council with his chief officers. With the fall of Vicksburg, Port Hudson was the last Confederate stronghold on the lower Mississippi River; surrendering it would mean to lose the river and all it had to give to the Union. Banks was demanding an unconditional surrender. Outside of this demand, there were few other options up for consideration. The Confederates could refuse to surrender, but that outlook was grim. The besieged men were already sick, wounded and near starvation. If they were to remain in the garrison, the situation stood only to deteriorate further. They were already surviving on weak beer and mule meat for rations. Even those poor provisions were only expected to last for a couple more weeks. The garrison would have a chance to survive if reinforcements and supplies were on their way, but they were not. Gardener was on his own. If surrendered, the garrison's men would be treated like prisoners of war, but at the very least, they would be provided with the medical attention many of them so badly needed.

Another fact that Gardner had to consider was that if he refused to surrender, the Yankees would certainly go ahead with their plan to blast Battery No. 11. By July 3, Bailey had begun digging a tunnel under the hill of the Citadel. At the end of that tunnel, Banks ordered 30 barrels of powder, which he planned to detonate on July 9. A second tunnel was also dug under Priest Cap, where 1,200 pounds of powder was placed. The plan was to detonate the powder under Priest Cap at the same time as the powder under

Battery No. 11. After simultaneously detonating both of the mines, the plan was to charge the two fortifications with his forlorn hope units, followed by the main army. Banks expected to be in full control of Port Hudson by the evening of July 9. When word came of Vicksburg's surrender, Banks abandoned the plan. Nevertheless, the powder still lay under the mines, ready to be ignited.

With no other viable solution at hand, the council reached its decision. At 2:00 a.m., Gardener sent a flag of truce to Banks. At 9:00 a.m. on July 8, Gardener sent Colonel Steedman, Colonel Miles and Lieutenant Colonel Smith to meet with General Stone, General Dwight and Colonel Birge of the Union. As the officials discussed the terms of the surrender, the ranks continued to fraternize with one another. Port Hudson returned to its commercial roots, even if it was only for a moment. As the two sides mingled, the Rebels and the Yankees traded with one another. While swapping goods and stories, the Confederates showed the Yankees around the garrison. They even went as far as to offer the Federal guests some of the weak corn beer that they had readily available. The show of hospitality was not isolated to the Confederates. The Union was just as hospitable and gave a tour of one of the war's most baffling projects, Bailey's Battery. Banks ordered food, along with medical supplies and a doctor, to be sent to the Confederates later on during the day on July 8. Upon arriving at the garrison, the Yankee doctor immediately tended to the sick and wounded. He even returned the following day to check up on his Southern patients.

As the doctor tended to the sick and wounded on the morning of July 9, the surrender ceremony was set to take place near the train depot. General Gardener rode along the line of the soldiers and patiently waited for the Union's arrival.

George L. Andrews.

The Federals arrived at the train depot with such fanfare that it could have been mistaken for a parade. General L. Andrews rode in with Birge's forlorn hope unit, regiments from other divisions and a series of bands playing loudly and proudly.

The ceremony was simple, civil and played out rather quickly. When Andrews approached Gardener, Gardener is quoted as saying, "Having thoroughly defended this position as long as I deemed it necessary I now surrender to you my sword and with it the post and its garrison." Andrews accepted the surrender but declined the sword. Andrews explained his refusal by stating, "I return your sword as a proper compliment to the gallant commander of such gallant—conduct that would be heroic in another cause."

The Confederate general gave the order for his men to ground arms, which they did without a word of disobedience. The Confederate flag was lowered, and the Union flag was raised in its place. Port Hudson officially belonged to the Union. After the ceremony, the ranks maintained their line. Most of them were prepared for the certainty of imprisonment that lay ahead for them. Therefore, one can imagine the excitement and celebration among the Rebel line when they were told they were going to be pardoned and allowed to go home.

The Siege of Port Hudson was the longest siege during the Civil War and cost both sides a tremendous loss. This is especially the case for the Union. From the firing of the first cannon during the initial Federal bombardment, Port Hudson endured for sixty-one days and was under siege for a total of forty-eight days. During this time, the Confederates lost an estimated 176 killed and 447 wounded. This number paled in comparison to the losses that General Banks sustained. The Union lost 4,363 men between May 23 and July 8. These losses included 45 officers killed and 191 wounded and 663 enlisted men killed, 3,145 wounded and 307 captured or missing. What was initially considered an outpost of the more formidable Vicksburg was able to outlast the Confederate stronghold. Even though this garrison was poorly manned, provisioned and armed, it managed to keep the Union army and navy at bay longer than any other fortification.

With the fall of Vicksburg and, ultimately, Port Hudson, the Union had successfully captured the last forty miles of the river needed to open it up. The war raged on and the Red River Campaign was in full swing, but the Confederacy did what it could to attempt to slow down the Union. The major battle dissipated in the region and the focus of the war moved west, but Confederate skirmishes and raids continued to plague the Union.

Chapter 23

The Battle of Kock's Plantation

Only days after the surrender of Port Hudson, Weitzel's and Grover's troops were sent to Donaldsonville. Once again, the little river town would experience military action. Each division positioned itself on either side of Bayou Lafourche. Even though the Federals had captured the Mississippi, they had yet to tame the interior of the region. Using Fort Butler as a base of operations, the goal was to capture Bayou Lafourche to support the Campaign on the Teche. Also, Brigadier General Thomas Green (CSA) was keeping a very close eye on the fort. In June, while most of the attention was given to Port Hudson, he attempted to take the fort but failed. Also in the area was Major's cavalry brigade. They were both tasked with the harassment of Union transport as they sailed upriver from New Orleans. The Confederates scattered themselves for nearly twenty miles along the banks of the Mississippi and stopped any Union boat from sailing farther than Donaldsonville. The only transports that could make it through were heavily armed and sustained heavy losses.

Upon the arrival of Weitzel and Grover, Major's brigade was recalled from the banks of the river and was repositioned on the banks of Bayou Lafourche. On the morning of July 13, Grover's men were on a foraging mission six miles south of Fort Butler, near Kock's Plantation. The Federals traveled down both sides of the bayou. N.A.M. Dudley marched down the west bank, while Colonel Joseph S. Morgan marched down the east bank. Morgan and his men first ran into Green's pickets, and skirmishing immediately ensued.

The Federals made several valiant attempts to make a stand, but Green consistently pushed them back. This was largely due to the efforts, or lack thereof, of Morgan. The acting brigadier had a history of drinking on duty and had even been accused of misdirecting an assault during the Siege of Port Hudson. Barely even a month after those accusations were made, it seemed as though Morgan was once again drunk while on duty. When the Rebels attacked, the foraging Yankees were caught by surprise. With no real leadership from their drunken colonel, the men pulled back and went into a full retreat. As Morgan's men retreated, Major's artillery took aim at Dudley's men on the west bank of the bayou, effectively pushing them back as well. The Confederates were able to push the Yankees back the full six miles to Fort Butler. However, once at Fort Butler, the Union had the protection of the heavy guns.

The Battle of Kock's Plantation was not only a clear victory for the Confederates, but it was also a victory that infuriated General Grover. The small force of 1,200 Rebel soldiers was able to push a Union force of nearly 4,000 back six miles while sustaining minimal losses. The small losses included 3 killed and 30 wounded. On the other hand, the Union sustained much larger losses: 56 killed, 217 wounded and 186 who were either captured or missing.

Colonel Joseph Morgan received most of the blame for the humiliating failure at Kock's Plantation and was court-martialed for "misbehavior before the enemy" and "drunkenness on duty." Though the Confederate victory was impressive, it was short-lived. Green had received word that two Union gunboats were headed to Berwick Bay. Green and his men pulled out of Donaldsonville and headed for the bay, where the battle for the Teche raged on.

Chapter 24

The Corps D'Afrique and the Battle at Centenary College

On May 1, 1863, Nathaniel Banks issued General Order No. 40, which proposed to organize an all-black corps of Union soldiers. The order stated, "It will consist ultimately of eighteen regiments, representing all arms—infantry, artillery, cavalry—making nine brigades of two regiments each, and three divisions of three brigades each, with appropriate corps of engineers, and flying hospitals for each division." Initially, the corps was an extension of the Louisiana Native Guard, a New Orleans militia group that was made up of freedmen of color. This group was expanded upon by adding former slaves who were conscripted into the war effort. By the start of the Siege of Port Hudson, the corps had grown into twenty regiments, divided into four brigades and two divisions, the whole under the command of Brigadier General G.L. Andrews and the first division commanded by Brigadier General Ullman of New York.

During the Siege of Port Hudson, these troops fought and contributed to the fall of the Confederate stronghold. Once the garrison fell, the corps remained stationed there to strengthen the works, erect an interior fort and participate in various skirmishes throughout the region. One such skirmish was the Battle at Jackson Crossroads.

Though they fought valiantly, the Corps D'Afrique did sustain some losses. Therefore, in an effort to build up the black regiment (mainly the Twelfth Regiment of the Corps D'Afrique), Andrews ordered a detachment of 300 African soldiers, 250 infantry and 50 cavalrymen from the Third Massachusetts, along with a section of Vermont Artillery. They were under the command of Lieutenant Moore Hanham and looking for freed or runaway slaves in the area to recruit into the corps. By some estimates, the detachment recruited nearly 50 men. However, these efforts were interrupted when the corps ran into Colonel John L. Logan and his 500 men near Jackson, Louisiana.

Logan commanded the Confederate cavalry and mounted infantry forces. He was stationed near Clinton, Louisiana, and often went up against Grierson and his Union cavalry. During the Siege of Port Hudson, he and his men had operated at the rear of the Union forces. The Confederate cavalry took the Corps D'Afrique by surprise on August 3, 1863, and fighting ensued.

The Federals made their stand near Centenary College, presently located in the heart of the city of Jackson. At present, the college is being maintained by the Office of Louisiana State Parks. The overall fight was brief. The corps was simply outmanned and was forced to retreat in a complete rout. Though the fighting was short-lived, Logan reported to have taken "two parrot guns, horses, ten wagons with commissary stores, killing wounding, and capturing not less than 100 Yankees and a large number of negroes in arms." Logan did not sustain nearly the losses of the Confederates. In his report, he stated that only twelve men were killed and wounded.

Centenary College is one of the oldest colleges in the state of Louisiana. It is actually the forty-third oldest college in the country, being founded in 1825. The students were primarily the children, primarily male, of planters and businessmen. During the 1840s, Centenary had established itself as one of the leading educational institutions in the country. The school's enrollment rivaled that of even Harvard. There were occasions when nearly three hundred students showed up for some sessions. However, the school's rural location in Jackson, Louisiana, along with a lack of financial support, caused it to lag behind. Nevertheless, the Civil War caused a lot more damage to Centenary than its location or lack of funds could ever inflict. Prior to the war, the school had boasted "a magnificent classroom/administration building," along with two dorms.

The college had a full enrollment up until the semester prior to the Civil War. During the war, the school closed its doors as a place of learning and reopened them as a place of healing. It was used as a military hospital for much of the war.

When the Civil War finally ended, the school tried once again to open its doors to the local students. However, the school, like much of the South, had a difficult time recovering from the war. Most of the buildings had taken a considerable amount of damage, and enrollment could never reach its prewar numbers. The college hobbled along until about 1908, when it moved to Shreveport, Louisiana. Only two buildings remain in Jackson: the West Wing Dormitory and the professor's house.

When rumors of the state's secession began to run rampant across Louisiana, it seems that most of the people in Pointe Coupee were ready to leave the Union. Even before state officials announced their declaration of secession, many men began organizing various regiments in preparation for the impending war. As early as November 1860, Samuel McKneely began organizing a cavalry regiment in the town of Livonia. Therefore, it is certainly no surprise that he was also one of the delegates who represented the parish in the Louisiana Secession Convention. The other delegate was Auguste Provosty. Obviously, both men were in favor of the state's secession. McKneely and Provosty were definitely not alone in their pro-secession sentiments. According to a January 4, 1861 issue of the *Pointe Coupee Democrat*, "We are proud to say that the wish for immediate secession appears to be as strong in the Parish as any other in the State. Men of all former parties are here joined heart and hand, none leading, in the holy work of preserving their incontestable rights."

Though these men were willing and able, the Federals did not make it to the area until August 1862. Even then, Yankee activity around Pointe Coupee only consisted of the Union navy sailing past the parish banks between Vicksburg and Baton Rouge. The closest these ships came to Pointe Coupee is when they stopped at Bayou Sara, across the river, to raid the port of coal and cotton.

The people of Pointe Coupee saw what these raids were doing to Bayou Sara and West Feliciana Parish as a whole. Therefore, to prevent the same activities from occurring in their parish, the militias and volunteer troops began to stand guard over key roads throughout the parish. They also attempted to guard or even hide sugar and cotton stores from the Union. However, in many cases it was not always feasible to fight for or hide these supplies, so sometimes the men were forced to destroy the valuable stores just to keep them out of the hands of the Yankees.

Chapter 25

Spring 1863

The spring of 1863 was a busy time in Pointe Coupee Parish. While much of the Confederate and Union focus was on Port Hudson and, farther north, Vicksburg, several small skirmishes broke out throughout the parish. One such skirmish occurred when Colonel Charles Paine ransacked the parish and arrested a priest. The priest, Father Francis Mittelbronn, was charged with blessing Confederate flags. Mittelbronn had been the chaplain for the Pointe Coupee Battery from the very beginning of the war. He even blessed the battery's flag before it marched on Vicksburg. However, during what became known as the Pointe Coupee Sacrilege, he was in the wrong place at the wrong time.

When the Yankees looted the area, they also vandalized graveyards and churches and destroyed many of the religious artifacts that they came across. Especially hard hit was Mittelbronn's own church, St. Francis Church of Pointe Coupee. Luckily for the father, he was not in his rectory when Paine and his men ransacked it. Mittelbronn, a strong supporter of the Confederacy, was transporting horses for the cause. Unfortunately for Mittelbronn, the Federals caught up with him and demanded that he turn over the horses to the Union. When the priest refused the Yankees' request, the horses were seized and he was arrested and imprisoned for ten days. When Mittelbronn finally returned to his church, he found it looted, vandalized and nearly destroyed.

Not even a month later, the Union came back. This time it was the crew of the *Switzerland*. The steamer docked at Taylor Landing and immediately began looting St. Francis Church. This went on for nearly two days. This

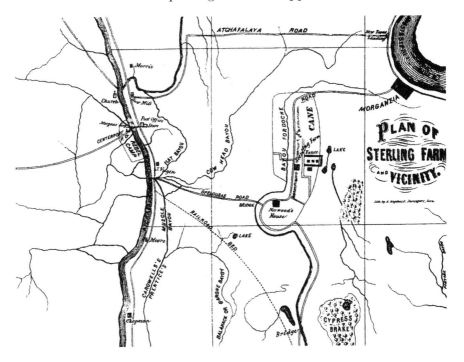

Battle of Stirling's Plantation.

time, though, the priest was left alone. No arrests were made. On the contrary, Admiral David Farragut made a public apology to the people of Pointe Coupee Parish. He also punished the crew of the *Switzerland* for their actions.

In an attempt to secure the interior west of the Mississippi River and to prevent the Confederates from having free reign in the upper portion of the Atchafalaya, the Union sent a 2,500-man division to Morganza, Louisiana. Major General N.J.T. Dana sent a detachment composed of Iowa, Indiana and Missouri infantry, along with two regiments of cavalry and a section of artillery, to Stirling's Plantation. This plantation was located along the road to the Atchafalaya Basin. The detachment, commanded by Colonel J.B. Leake, was tasked with repelling the Confederates. A day later, Leake got the opportunity to repel those forces.

On the morning of September 29, around 1:00 a.m., General Thomas Green reached the east bank of the Atchafalaya with two cavalry battalions and Semmes's battery. By daybreak, the regiment had divided into two detachments. Mouton's and Spieghts's infantry brigade navigated through the swamp, making their way to a road that ran right behind the plantation. Meanwhile, Green marched up the main road with the rest of the troops toward Fordouche Bridge. It seems Green laid a trap for the Federals.

Around lunchtime, Green's men reached the bridge and a Union picket stationed there. The forces clashed, and skirmishing immediately broke out. During the fighting, Stirling's Plantation burst into flames. The Confederates were able to push back the Yankees. A mile from the bridge, a Confederate cavalry battalion, led by Major L.C. Roundtree, met with the Federal cavalry line ready for battle. The plan was to push the Yankees into the infantry brigade lying in wait behind Stirling's Plantation. Roundtree ordered his men to charge, effectively scattering the Union cavalry. Though some captures were made, overall, most of the Union troops escaped down a narrow road that the Rebels seemed to have overlooked.

The skirmish was a Confederate victory. The Union lost 66 men killed or wounded and 462 captured. Aside from the Yankee prisoners, the Rebels also gained a fair amount of spoils, which included two ten-pound Parrott guns, two ambulances, a medical wagon and a large cache of medical supplies. Though Green had won the day, it did not effectively slow the Union. Nathaniel Banks continued to force his way up the region toward Texas.

Chapter 26

The Yankees Go West

After the surrender of Port Hudson, the Civil War in the lower Mississippi region became less intense. The Rebels and the Yankees still faced off; however, these could barely be considered battles or even skirmishes. Most of the activities in the region were quick raids on camps, guerrilla activity and small engagements. Nevertheless, the war was not over. It simply moved upriver. The Union had set its sights on the Confederate capital of Louisiana, Shreveport. From 1862, when the Union occupied Baton Rouge, the state's capital was moved several times, first to Opelousas and then to north Louisiana. By 1864, it was settled in Shreveport in an effort to keep it out of the hands of the Federals. Once the Union controlled the Mississippi River from its mouth in the Gulf of Mexico past Port Hudson up to Vicksburg, they focused on the Red River region of Louisiana.

The Red River Campaign was a two-fold expedition. Not only were the Federals trying to gain control of the capital in Louisiana, but they were also attempting to control the Red River to the north, along with the interior of east Texas. Acquiring these two objectives would solidify the Union's presence in Louisiana and leave little room for the Confederates to regain control. Unfortunately for the Union, they were not successful. The Red River Campaign was a miserable failure for the Federals. It was poorly planned and executed.

Though this maneuver did not do much in the way of opening the Mississippi River back up to the Confederates, it did keep Louisiana from completely falling to General Nathaniel Banks. Overall, the only other accomplishment that can be credited to the Red River Campaign was extending the Civil War for another year. As for the lower Mississippi River, the Union maintained control of the region until the end of the war.

Following the Red River Campaign, the Union troops retreated back to Morganza, Louisiana, in Pointe Coupee Parish. Immediately, they began constructing fortifications while Banks planned his next move. Once again, the Union looted Pointe Coupee Parish in an effort to collect enough rations and supplies to build its defensive structure. In some cases, the Union did not only loot but demolished as well. After the war was over, a planter woman by the name of Fannie Riche filed a claim against the U.S. government. The claim stated that not only did Banks's men confiscate livestock and building materials, but they even went as far as to tear down her kitchen building and house on her property and steal any usable building materials.

This Federal activity attracted a number of Confederate cavalrymen and a series of raids and skirmishes. Confederate captain Emile Carmouche led several of these raids during the fall of 1864. During a skirmish at LaCoste's Plantation on November 2, Carmouche and his men were able to push back a Federal force of 150 men, killing 10, while the Confederates only lost 2 men to capture and no casualties. Skirmishes such as these did little to help the Confederate cause, but they did slow the Federal movement in Pointe Coupee.

By December 1864, most of the action in the parish had come to a halt. The Union still maintained the fort in Morganza, but the number of troops stationed there was vastly reduced. Only on occasion after 1864 did the Union troops take any action. On the rare occasion that they did conduct a mission, it was basically just a show of force to remind the Rebels that the Union still occupied the area. For all practical purposes, the Civil War in Pointe Coupee ended in 1864. It, too, was lost to the Union, just like the other parishes along the Mississippi River that fell before it.

Conclusion

The fight to capture the lower Mississippi River is often summarized with the two major battles in the area: the Battle of Baton Rouge and the Siege of Port Hudson. However, the area was plagued with a series of smaller battles that were oftentimes just a show of force. These smaller battles did nothing to further the cause of either side. Instead, the only discernible outcome was the loss of life on the part of the Union and the Confederacy. Though the campaign to control the Mississippi River was vital to both Rebel and Yankee, it was filled with contradiction.

In many cases, especially with the surrender of New Orleans, a single shot was not even fired. Even though most of the action took place on the river near Forts Jackson and St. Philip, New Orleans did not see any fighting. The Federals were able to dock their ships and simply occupy New Orleans with very little resistance. It is baffling to realize that one of the most important cities in the South was taken without a fight. This is arguably the turning point in the fight for the Mississippi River. If the Confederacy could have held on to New Orleans, it may have had a fighting chance to maintain some control of the river. At the very least, the city could have acted as a Confederate hub to transport men and supplies by river and rail. Nevertheless, the Union took the city and all its strategic value.

Yet the tiny town of Donaldsonville, Louisiana, was not spared. The town was flattened not for supplies or strategy but for revenge. The Union used the town to set an example. When Confederates refused to stop firing on passing Union ships, the Union took action. The only buildings allowed to stand after the Yankee bombardment were the town's church and the attached orphanage. That was only the first indignity the town was forced to suffer. A year later, when the Confederates attempted to take Fort Butler, they were not allowed to bury their dead. Many of the fallen men were tossed in a single mass grave almost lost to history.

The city of Baton Rouge held no real strategic value, but in the end it was nearly obliterated as well. It was not a major commercial port during the time of the Battle of Baton Rouge, and its position on the river was too difficult to defend. It was not even a political victory due to the fact that the state capital had been moved to Opelousas prior to the Union's arrival. Once again, its only real objective was to prove that the Union could not only take the city but continue to occupy it. After the Battle of Baton Rouge, the Yankees did not stay. Almost immediately, the men boarded their ships and moved on to areas they believed to be more important, such as Vicksburg and Port Hudson.

Just up the river, Port Hudson's position on the river was just as valuable as Vicksburg, but it was doomed from the start because of the Confederate bureaucracy. One of the Confederacy's most strategic points on the Mississippi River was undermanned, undersupplied and poorly armed. Yet the Confederate troops stationed there were able to maintain their position longer than Vicksburg, which was better supplied, manned and armed. This became such an issue for the Confederates that they began to hold the newly formed government in contempt.

As for the bustling town of Bayou Sara, it, too, was leveled. The town's position was not as valuable as Port Hudson and it was not a center of commerce, like New Orleans. However, if the town had not been plagued with raids and bombardments, it possibly could have grown into an important trade hub on the river. This was largely due to its connection to Woodville, Mississippi, the cotton hub of the region. This could be why the town became a favorite raiding spot for the Federals. It seems that when the U.S. Navy was sailing to or from Vicksburg, it would stop in Bayou Sara for supplies or coal, whether the locals liked it or not. Unfortunately for Bayou Sara, the Civil War was not the only plague the town had to deal with. After the war, Bayou Sara suffered several natural disasters and fires, which all but destroyed what the War Between the States had left behind. The town never returned to its former self and retreated into the town of St. Francisville, one mile from the banks of the river and positioned on bluffs.

It could easily be argued that if the Confederates could have kept these points along the Mississippi they could have maintained control of the river itself. However, the fact remains that they could do little to stop the Federal advance up the river. With Vicksburg and Port Hudson falling to the Union virtually at the same time, the Anaconda Plan was complete. The Union successfully captured the Mississippi River.

Bibliography

Abraham Lincoln Online. "First Inaugural Address. March 4, 1861. Washington, D.C." showcase.netins.net/web/creative/lincoln/speeches/1inaug.htm.

American Civil War Stories. "Fort Butler—Donaldsonville, Louisiana, the Forgotten Fort." civilwarstories.blogspot.com/2008/06/fort-butler-donaldsonville-louisiana.html.

Anaconda Plan. www.mycivilwar.com/campaigns/610400.htm.

Bache, Alexander D. *Report of the Superintendent of the Coast Survey, Showing the Progress of the Survey During the Year 1862*. Appendix No 35. "Report of Assistant F.H. Gerdes, U.S. Coast Survey, to Commander D.D. Porter, U.S.N., Commanding Mortar Flotilla in the Gulf of Mexico," 263.

Baton Rouge Weekly Gazette & Comet. "Now Then, What Next?" February 2, 1861, 1.

Bergeron, Arthur W., Jr. *The Louisiana Purchase Bicentennial Series in Louisiana History*. Vol. 5, part A. Lafayette: Center for Louisiana Studies University of Louisiana at Lafayette, 2002.

Boynton, Charles. *History of the Navy*. New York: D. Appleton and Company, 1868.

Bradshaw, Jim. "Battle of Baton Rouge." KnowLA Encyclopedia of Louisiana. www.knowla.org/entry.php?rec=560.

Brown, Dee. *Grierson's Raid: A Cavalry Adventure of the Civil War*. IL: University of Illinois Press, 1962.

BrownWater Navy. "West Gulf Blockading Squadron (Operations on the Mississippi River)." www.brownwaternavy.org/lmiss.htm.

The Burning of Bayou Sara. historyengine.richmond.edu/episodes/view/4127.

Civil War Reference. "Amite River." www.civilwarreference.com/battles/detail.php?battlesID=1483.

———. "George Nichols Hollins." www.civilwarreference.com/people/index.php?peopleID=2092.

Civil War Talk. "Battle of Baton Rouge." civilwartalk.com/forums/showthread.php?49795-Battle-of-Baton-Rouge.

Civil War Wiki. "Battle of Plains Store." civilwarwiki.net/wiki/Battle_of_Plains_Store.

Cormier, Steven A. "1st Regiment Volunteer Cavalry." www.acadiansingray.com/1st%20Regt.%20Cav.htm.

Costello, Brian J. *A History of Pointe Coupee Parish, Louisiana.* LA: Margaret Media, 2010.

Dawson, Sarah Morgan. *Confederate Girl's Diary.* NJ: Touchtone, 1992.

Dinges, Bruce J. "America's Civil War: Colonel Benjamin Grierson's Cavalry Raid in 1863." *Civil War Times Magazine*, February 1996.

Ella and Annie. www.history.navy.mil/photos/sh-civil/civsh-e/ella-ann.htm.

Estaville, Lawrence E. "A Small Contribution: Louisiana's Short Rural Railroads in the Civil War." *Louisiana History: The Journal of the Louisiana Historical Association* 18, no. 1 (Winter 1977): 87–103.

Explore Southern History. "Port Hudson State Historic Site." www.exploresouthernhistory.com/porthudson.html.

Faust, Patricia L. *Historical Times Encyclopedia of the Civil War.* New York: Harper Perennial, 1991.

Fort Butler: Donaldson, LA. www.civilwaralbum.com/louisiana/donaldsonville.htm.

Guillory, Rev. Fr. Brad D. "Connections in Stone." www.stmarymagdalenparish.org/connections-in-stone.

Haase, Carol K. *Louisiana Old State Capitol.* LA: Pelican Publishing Co., 2009.

history.latech.edu/publications/conf%20long%20desc.htm.

Hunter, G. Howard. "Fall of New Orleans and Federal Occupation." KnowLA Encyclopedia of Louisiana. www.knowla.org/entry.php?rec=776.

Johnson, Robert Underwood, and Johnson Buel. *Battles and Leaders of the Civil War.* Vol. 1. New York: Century Co., 1887.

Judgment Day. "The Civil War and Emancipation." www.pbs.org/wgbh/aia/part4/4p2967.html.

Lester, C.E. "The Gunboat Essex." *Harper's New Monthly Magazine*, February 1863. www.navyandmarine.org/ondeck/186Essex.htm.

Life on the Mississippi. New York: Houghton and Company, 1874. Chap. 40, 416–17. Digital version on "Documents of the American South," University of North Carolina at Chapel Hill.

Louisiana's Military Heritage: Vessels Named USS Barataria. www.usskidd. com/ships-barataria.html.

LSU Libraries, Special Collections. "Occupation, Battle, and Aftermath." www.lib.lsu.edu/special/exhibits/e-exhibits/Lytle/battle.html.

Mooney, James L. Dictionary of American Naval Fighting Ships. "Barataria." March 6, 2006. www.history.navy.mil/danfs/b2/barataria-i.htm.

Morgan, Dr. Lee. "A Brief History of Centenary College of Louisiana." www.centenary.edu/about/history.

National Park Service. "The Civil War in the Lower Mississippi River Valley." www.nps.gov/history/delta/civil_war/index.htm.

————. "Plains Store." www.nps.gov/hps/abpp/battles/la009.htm.

Ordinances of Secession. Official Records, Ser. IV, vol. 1. www.constitution. org/csa/ordinances_secession.htm.

Pardue, D.N. "Bayou Sara—Town and Stream." files.usgwarchives.org/la/ westfeliciana/history/bsarah.txt.

Pena, Christopher G. "The Day the War Stopped: The Truth Revealed." www.daythewarstopped.net/truthrevealed.html.

Pierson, Michael D. *Mutiny at Fort Jackson: The Untold Story of the Fall of New Orleans*. Chapel Hill: University of North Carolina Press, 2008.

Richey, Thomas H. *The Battle of Baton Rouge*. TX: VirtualBookWorm.com Publishing, 2005.

Rickard, J. "Battle of Baton Rouge, 5 August 1862." June 1, 2007. www. historyofwar.org/articles/battles_baton_rouge.html.

Ripley, Eliza Moore Chinn McHatton. "From Flag to Flag: A Woman's Adventures and Experiences in the South during the War, in Mexico, and in Cuba." docsouth.unc.edu/fpn/ripleyflag/ripley.html.

Roland, Charles Pierce. *Louisiana Sugar Plantations During the Civil War*. Baton Rouge: Louisiana State University Press, Shields, Richard E., Jr. "Freemasonry During Wartime." www.masonicworld.com/education/ files/artoct02/freemasonry_during_wartime.htm.

The 6th Massachusetts Light Artillery Service Record. www.oocities.org/ heartland/woods/3501/service1.htm.

Special Correspondent from the Delta. "From New Orleans." *New York Times*, August 30, 1862. www.nytimes.com/1862/08/30/news/ important-new-orleans-operations-against-guerrillas-mississippi-abandonment.html.

Spedale, W.A. *Battle of Baton Rouge 1862*. LA: Land and Land Publishing, 1985.

———. *Fort Butler 1863*. Donaldsonville, LA, 1997.

United States War Dept. *Official Records of the Union and Confederate Navies in the War of the Rebellion*. ORN I, vol. 18, 373. Washington, D.C.: Government Printing Office, n.d.

———. *The War of the Rebellion: A Compilation of the Official Records of the Union and Confederate Armies*. Ser. 1, vol. 15. Washington, D.C.: Government Printing Office, 1886.

Winters, John D. *The Civil War in Louisiana*. Baton Rouge: Louisiana State University Press, 1991.

Wright, Howard C. *Port Hudson: Its History from an Interior Point of View*. St. Francisville, LA, 1937. Repr., Baton Rouge, LA: Eagle Press, 1978.

Index

About the Author

For nearly a decade, Dennis John Dufrene has worked in the field of history. While earning a bachelor of arts degree in the field of history from Nicholls State University, Dennis completed a plantation internship at Laura Valley Plantation. This internship allowed him to perfect his researching skills and learn the importance of preserving and maintaining collections of historic artifacts.

After graduation, Dennis married his wife, Tweety, and the couple moved to St. Francisville, Louisiana. It was during this time that Dennis was hired as an interpretive ranger at Audubon State Historic Site, also known as Oakley Plantation. Dennis began to write numerous history-based articles and press releases, give lectures, create exhibits, etc. Many of his articles were published, and he was even credited as a source in the book *A Summer of Birds* by Danny Heitman.

Following the birth of their son, Myles, the couple moved, and Dennis began a career in technical writing; however, his passion for history never wavered. In his spare time, he served as senior writer for a historical conspiracy website known as Top Secret Writers. Each week, he wrote a series of articles and blogs on various history happenings.

In the winter of 2011, Dennis jumped at the chance to write his first book on the Civil War from a local perspective. For nearly a year, he conducted research and met with local experts to compile his latest work. It was during this time that he learned about the intricate role that the Civil War played on shaping the Baton Rouge area.

Even though Dennis's career path has veered slightly away from the field of history, his passion and love of the subject matter have remained unchanged. He continues to try to find ways to learn more about and work (indirectly) in the field by writing articles and researching various events.